Content is King: Writing and Editing Online

Content is King: Writing and Editing Online

David Mill

Routledge
Taylor & Francis Group
LONDON AND NEW YORK

First published 2005 by Butterworth-Heinemann

2 Park Square, Milton Park, Abingdon, Oxon OX14 4RN
711 Third Avenue, New York, NY 10017, USA

Routledge is an imprint of the Taylor & Francis Group, an informa business

First issued in hardback 2016

British Library Cataloguing in Publication Data
A catalogue record for this book is available from the British Library

Library of Congress Control Number: 2005922525

ISBN-13: 978-0-7506-6317-5 (pbk)
ISBN-13: 978-1-138-15058-4 (hbk)

Contents

Preface

Some years before Tim Berners-Lee invented the World Wide Web, I was serving my early apprenticeship in journalism as a junior sub-editor on a national weekly newspaper.

At that time, we had **typewriters**, **hot metal** and **ink**.

In the 25 or so years since, I have been fortunate to participate in the ever-changing face of publishing from mainframe direct-entry computer systems to desktop publishing to satellite printing to web publishing.

And, while it's a blessing to no longer go home with the day's headlines printed on my forearms (from leaning on the 'stone' while trying to read the inked typeset lines in reverse), one thing has never changed . . .

. . . the craft of writing.

My professional bible in those early days was *The Simple Subs Book*, which was written in 1968 by Leslie Sellers, the then Production editor of the *Daily Mail*.

Within it, there is a series of questions that every writer and editor should ask themselves about a piece of work:

1. **Are the facts right?**
2. **Are there any loose ends?**
3. **Is everything clear?**
4. **Does it flow like honey, or does it stick in the craw?**
5. **Does it make any unnecessary demands on the reader?**
6. **Can it be simplified?**

We can, indeed, learn from the past as those rules still apply today. Perhaps even more so when the short attention span of the average online reader is considered.

The secret of good writing is to say an old thing in a new way or to say a new thing in an old way.

—Richard Harding Davis

And, in relation to online content, Mr Sellers might well have added that good copywriting has to pass the AIDAS test . . .

grabbing	**Attention**
strengthening	**Interest**
stimulating	**Desire**
encouraging	**Action**
delivering	**Satisfaction**

My own newspaper path included the *Daily Record*, *Sunday Mail*, the *Evening Times*, the *Evening News* and *The Mercury* (Australia) as well as projects for *The People* and *The Independent* and an award-winning period as launch Editor of *The Glaswegian*, then the UK's most widely distributed free newspaper and the first to be published using Apple Macs and QuarkXPress.

With the latter I was fortunate to pick up many national awards including ones for Editorial Excellence as well as Best Design and the main honour of UK Newspaper of the Year.

And, while successes were due to a number of factors, the approach was always to begin with the questions:

- Who?
- What?
- When?
- Where?
- Why?
- How?

Good newspaper articles begin by answering most of these questions. And they can also be applied to larger editorial projects, design initiatives and, of course, **online copywriting** and **editing**.

In relation to applying that offline knowledge and experience into New Media, my own first taste of using online content came about in an unusual way.

I'd just completed a mammoth project, then as Production Editor, of introducing new technology into Mirror Group's *Daily Record* and *Sunday Mail*, replacing traditional publishing systems and practices with Apple Macs, desktop scanners, an electronic picture desk and more.

Looking back, it was probably that which opened my eyes to the **power of electronic publishing**.

For example, while it had previously taken a large team to produce the content and pages on the night of a General Election, in 1983 that team became just me on an Apple Mac (oh, I loved it so) supported by a single programmer (they may speak Klingon but I accept they're truly gifted!).

Anyway, after the project was completed and just as I was drawing breath, I received a call from a colleague, Elsa McAlonan, who at the time of writing is Editor of *Woman's Own*. She had been drafted in to a hush-hush Mirror Group project and had been asked to invite me to participate.

The project? David Montgomery, then Chief Executive of the Mirror Group, wanted to launch a **new middle-market newspaper**, code-named *Newsday*, and its first copies were to be created and then published in Scotland prior to a proposed national launch.

Next thing I knew I was holed up in a hotel outside Glasgow with Elsa and three executives who had been dispatched from London – David Banks (Editorial Director and former Editor of the *Daily Mirror*), Pat Pilton (Editorial Manager and, the last I heard, Director of Editorial Operations at the Press Association) and Len Gould (who went on to edit *The People*).

My task was to create a design for the newspaper, edit the first drafts and create a production platform. But there was a problem – **we had no content**!

And the project was so secret I couldn't communicate with my colleagues at the *Daily Record* and *Sunday Mail*.

But, ah ha, I had heard of **CompuServe**! So I opened an account, bought a modem (yes, crawling along at 9.6 kbps) and voila! I was able to **download content** and photographs from other newspaper archives for use within the draft pages.

Sadly, a distracting newspaper price war then broke out and, as a result, the only final copies of the *Newsday* pages that were ever seen were outputted to a laser printer in a purpose-built office that was only ever occupied by David Banks and me!

But . . . I'd seen the light and the CompuServe experience quickly led me to this thing called the **Internet** and a knocking at the door of the Managing Director, Kevin Beatty (who later headed up Associated Newspapers' new media operations and, the last I heard, is managing director of Northcliffe Newspapers).

I had said 'Kevin, we really need to be part of the Internet and the Web. It's the future of publishing', or something along these lines.

And so it came to pass. This time hidden away on an executive floor, I taught myself HTML, designed and built a *Daily Record* and *Sunday Mail* website and launched it as the **UK's first online tabloid** (only the *Electronic Telegraph* pipped us to the post as the first UK newspaper online).

And here is how it was announced (my first taste of what we now call Internet marketing):

News: Britain's first national tabloid newspaper on the WWW
Forum: HyperNews Guestbook
From: David Mill <dmill@record-mail.co.uk>

The first British national tabloid newspaper to be published on the WWW is the *Daily Record* and *Sunday Mail*.

http://www.record-mail.co.uk/rm/
or
http://www.cityscape.co.uk/rm/

It contains News, Sport, Features and a Magazine section as well as Tourism information, Historical information, Telephone Dating, Competitions, Cartoons, Crossword, Agony Aunt, Picture Gallery and much more.

Thought you might like to have a look and I'd welcome your comments.

Thanks.

And I had a new job title: Online Editor. Some of my colleagues at the time cautioned me. 'It's like CB Radio,' they said, 'a passing fad.'

But I thought differently and so did David Banks, who shared the vision and assisted my passage to London where I became Group Online Editor of Mirror Group. From those lofty floors in Canary Wharf the first **electronic editions** of Mirror Group's titles began to appear, starting with *The Sporting Life*.

And, yes, for those who remember, I was also responsible for launching *L!ve TV* online – complete with topless darts and the rabbit newsreader. Sorry about that!

However, that distraction aside, my own belief was that Mirror Group should not simply repurpose print content for publication online. Rather, I believed it should also take selected content from its various channels and create **a new online brand**, which I labelled *MegaNet*.

This would, according to my then future-thinking plan, have existing content edited specifically for the Web and custom content created for the online readership. And it was a step ahead of the information portals that were to follow.

But something called AOL came along and, for me, everything changed.

AOL had few content sources when it launched in the UK and, after participating in long hours of negotiation, I found myself party to an agreement which would see my team change focus – to become key content providers for the online service.

There was no content management system in those days. This was raw cut-and-paste from the desktop publishing system into the AOL templates, on-the-fly editing and through-the-night working.

Great early experience of preparing content for online readers in a certain form but a relentless effort which also distracted attention from the larger opportunity – the Internet.

Therefore, eventually, David Banks and I took another diversion which saw us setting up what was then Media.Co.Uk Ltd and led to me giving up the 20 or so years in the newspaper world to focus independently on online initiatives.

Web development, consultancy, **online content editing** and **copywriting** . . . not many people were doing that at the time (not enough are doing it well even now!). And, with clients like Ladbrokes, it was an early success story.

However, once more, a new Internet opportunity arrived at my doorstep. Scotland On Line came calling and tempted me with a great challenge – to lead the further development of the online Gateway to Scotland and establish it as the 'definitive Internet source of all things Scottish'.

At that time, Scotland On Line (www.scotlandonline.com) was the joint initiative of ScottishTelecom (now Thus) and D.C. Thomson (famously publishers of *The Sunday Post* and *The Beano*).

And, during my two years or so as Head of Publishing and Content, page views were increased some 700 per cent.

Scottish news, sport, football, tartans, travel . . . even a web cam on Loch Ness for those global monster spotters! It was a great train set and a wonderful opportunity to develop and present content ideally suited to the online readership.

One of the email newsletters also helped us win a **national new media award** ahead of entries from the BBC and *The Guardian* . . . happy days.

However, in 1999, having been there, done that and had the T-shirts printed, I decided to leave Scotland On Line to its own devices and venture again into independent territory.

Since then, it's been MediaCo (Internet marketing, web publishing and content development) and, of course, this book . . ..

So, enough about me . . . let's put **you** and **your readers** into the action . . ..

The purpose of **Content is King** (Writing and Editing Online) is to help you to **write**, **edit** and **publish** more effective content for your online readership.

Whether you're a **marketer**, **editor** or **copywriter**, I hope you will find it helpful, on an ongoing basis, to weave your words in such a way as to consistently satisfy your online audience and achieve your particular objectives.

Words are the most powerful drug used by mankind.

— Rudyard Kipling

Acknowledgements

At first, this appeared to be the most difficult part to write. It was, therefore, left blank until near the end. Then I realized it was a particularly personal opportunity I may never have again.

No, not to lavishly thank Dave Chaffey, the series editor (whose own book, *Total E-mail Marketing*, is an excellent part of this collection) and who, in any case, already has my gratitude.

Nor to make mention of the many talented, funny and often eccentric content creators and editors it has been my greatest fortune to work with and learn from – total respect (sorry Ken T, I do now know 'total' is a redundant word!).

But, rather, to make two important acknowledgements. Of . . .

1. The Alzheimer's Society.
   The care and research charity for people with dementia, their families and carers. You can make your donations with mine at:
   http://www.alzheimers.org.uk/

2. Primarily, my Mum.
   Because, while she is now in a different zone – distanced, particularly from the family she cherishes – and whether or not this book is considered to be good, bad or indifferent, she'd be proud of me for writing (and getting to the end of) it. And woe betold any reviewer who criticized it!

   So, thank you, Mum – Frances Simpson Mill – the great many games of Scrabble and countless crossword challenges must have contributed, too.

And this is probably an indulgence, she (and, I hope, you) would forgive!

There is a time for many words, and there is also a time for sleep.

—Homer

So let's enjoy this time and our words . . . and try to make them better than simply good enough . . ..

Introduction – Content is Still King

In 1997, web usability expert Jakob Nielsen began one of his well-read articles with the words:

How Users Read on the Web . . .
. . . **they don't**.

Okay, so if correct, you might well conclude that's the end of the story and the rest of this book is really about the meaning of life and other unrelated ramblings. **Not!**

Of course, we **do read** on the web. But we read in a **different manner** to the way we consume printed material.

And, to be fair to Jakob, he did go on to say: 'People rarely read web pages word by word; instead, they scan the page, picking out individual words and sentences.'

'In a *recent study, John Morkes and I found that 79 per cent of our test users always scanned any new page they came across; only 16 per cent read word-by-word.'

So there we have it. The secret to success is to solely present a series of buzz words and attention-grabbing sentences.

Well, no. Of course, that's not the case either.

But, in almost every case of **writing and editing** for the online readership, text should be:

- Concise;
- Credible; and, indeed
- Scannable.

This, you will find, is a recurring theme throughout the course of this book. Other areas we will cover in detail include:

- Interactivity
- Personality
- Tone and style.

And the **main aim** will be to help you to:

- Say the **right** thing
- In the **right** way
- To the **right** person.

NOTE Each chapter closes with a checklist and all the checklists are repeated at the end of the book. I hope you will find them to be a useful addition to your online writer's toolkit.

Good writing is clear thinking made visible.

— Bill Wheeler

*Tourist attractions in Nebraska were the subject of the Nielsen and Morkes study. While it could be argued material of this nature is more likely to be scanned than read in full, the test – and experience – indicates that **scannable text** is, without doubt, best if it's being prepared for presentation to the general online readership.

Web link

Jakob Nielsen's Alert Boxes
http://www.useit.com/alertbox/

CHAPTER 1 Copywriting for Online Versus Offline

Overview

Copywriting for online readership requires an approach different from creating content intended for publication in print, whether being newly created or being re-purposed from existing material.

Copy length, pointers and links, typographic styles, interaction – these are among the items that require alternative treatment.

Chapter objectives

Through this chapter, you will discover the differences between how people read on screen and print.

You will also gain an understanding of how to create effective copy for the online readership, including writing styles, interactivity and relationship building.

Chapter structure

- Introduction – readers and skimmers
- Less is more – bytes and pieces
- Start Here – entry points
- Get to the point – pyramid style
- Bite the bullets – plus links, headings and sub-headings
- Accessibility
- Interactivity
- The one-to-one relationship
- Summary
- Checklist.

Introduction – readers and skimmers

When we write for print, we expect the reader to closely follow our copy from start to finish, following the logical path of our presentation.

However, as we recognized in this book's introduction, the online reader tends to **skim and scan content**. In addition, they will most often jump from **item to item**, **page to page** (which is what hyperlinks are for, after all).

NOTE

Skimming is when a reader quickly runs their eyes over your text to identify the main ideas presented.

Scanning is when they are running their eyes over the text and picking out specific words or phrases – either ones they are seeking or ones you have drawn to their attention through text styling.

The online copywriter, therefore, has to ensure:

- key content is quickly and easily consumed
- the most important information is near the start of the copy
- content is organized in an easy-to-follow and intuitive navigational structure.

to:

- enhance the readers' experience
- keep them on-site
- successfully gain the desired actions
- deliver the objectives.

Less is more – bytes and pieces

As if skimming and jumping around wasn't enough to cope with, it's also important to appreciate that web readers simply do not like long sections of copy (deep scrolling), particularly within the upper and introductory levels of content.

Therefore, content should be broken up into **smaller, logically organized sections**. Plus, since reading from a screen is somewhat painful compared with print, the **less is more** rule should be followed, with copy length being as condensed as possible – perhaps **half the length** and broken up into chunks.

Also, you should endeavour to:

- keep sentences to **about 15–25 words in length**
- use **one idea** per sentence
- include a sentence at or near the start of each paragraph that **conveys the point** of the whole paragraph.

This will deliver benefits to the scanning reader (who often only reads the first part of a paragraph to assess whether it's relevant to them) and will enhance understanding (since the point of the paragraph is made clear at the outset)

- bear in mind that paragraphs are optimally no more than **four sentences** and preferably two in length (ideally, **two or three lines** deep)
- use paragraphs that only contain sentences that relate to each other, with each paragraph serving a **particular purpose**. The scanning reader sees paragraphs as individual elements and you will, therefore, gain more if each paragraph presents a separate point.

Also, while it most likely will be a natural style if you are writing in a conversational manner, you should use **transitional expressions** and **hooks** to establish logical connections between paragraphs.

A transitional expression between paragraphs can, at its simplest, be a few words at the beginning of the paragraph following.

For example:

- accordingly
- after a while
- after all
- also
- and
- as a result
- as has been said
- at that time
- besides
- despite
- earlier
- elsewhere
- finally
- for all that
- for instance
- furthermore
- however
- in addition
- in brief
- in conclusion
- in contrast
- in fact
- in other words
- in particular
- in the meantime

- indeed
- of course
- on the contrary
- on the other hand
- on the whole
- similarly
- still
- subsequently
- then
- therefore

and

- for example [!].

And simple hooks include:

- **The last word hook:**

  Use transitional expressions and hooks to establish logical connections between paragraphs.

  <u>Paragraphs</u> should be . . .
- **The last sentence hook:**

  As we recognized in this book's introduction, the online reader tends to skim content. In addition, they will most often jump from item to item, page to page (which is what hyperlinks are for, after all).

  When a reader jumps from <u>item to item</u> it should be remembered . . .
- **The deeper hook:**

  Use transitional expressions and hooks to establish logical connections between paragraphs.

  It is important, <u>however</u>, to ensure . . .

- **The idea hook** (this refers to an idea just expressed):

  Since reading from a screen is somewhat painful compared with print, the less is more rule should be followed.

  Such a view might seem alien to those who believe quality is measured on quantity.

EXAMPLE

From startups.co.uk's *Startup* guides:

There are few things more tempting than the smell of fish and chips.

So the idea of owning your own fish and chip shop will probably seem like a similarly alluring prospect.

Don't fall into the nostalgia trap, though, this isn't Last of the Summer Wine. The modern day takeaway has big competition so you need to put a lot in to get it right.

Get the winning formula, however, and you'll soon be cashing in your chips.

In the past few years, there has been a pretender to the throne of Britain's favourite takeaway, chicken tikka masala. However, traditionalists can now breathe a sigh of relief: fish and chips is firmly back on top according to a recent survey by the British Potato council.

But its place there isn't down to traditional values. This market of independents has enjoyed leading the field for much of the first 100 years of its history. Gradually, the customer has been faced with a large number of alternatives, from Chinese to burgers, Indian to pizza.

Increasingly, fish shops can't just open when they please and customers will vote against poor quality with their feet. This isn't consistent throughout the industry, however, so a good business will have its own very high standards.

Broadly, it's about brighter, spotlessly clean shops, well-trained and pleasant staff, good economic practices – and most importantly a flawless product. Vinegar soaked newspaper wrapping no longer meets customer expectations and when 70 to 80% of your business is repeat, this is very important.

And it's important to make the most of the product you have.

---

http://www.startups.co.uk/

But don't force it. This is **not essential** for every paragraph and, if it feels uncomfortable when you read it back, it is! Rules are meant to be broken and the best medicine is always taken or served in moderation.

In addition, your reader will not appreciate any form of verbosity, the use of an excessive number of words. So try to avoid writing, for example, '**a large number of**' when '**many**' will do or '**despite the fact that**' instead of '**although**'.

Writing less is, in any case, also much more effective – and often more difficult to create – in any medium.

As others have said:

- *If I had more time, I would have written a shorter letter.*

  — Marcus T. Cicero

- *Brevity is the soul of wit.*

  — William Shakespeare

- *Not that the story need be long, but it will take a long while to make it short.*

  — Henry David Thoreau

- *You know that I write slowly. This is chiefly because I am never satisfied until I have said as much as possible in a few words, and writing briefly takes far more time than writing at length.*

  — Karl Friedrich Gauss

- *It is my ambition to say in 10 sentences what others say in a whole book.*

  — Nietzsche

- *The more you say, the less people remember. The fewer the words, the greater the profit.*

  — Felelon

- *My aim is to put down on paper what I see and what I feel in the best and simplest way.*

  — Ernest Hemingway.

- *Vigorous writing is concise. A sentence should contain no unnecessary words, a paragraph no unnecessary sentences, for the same reason that a drawing should have no unnecessary lines and a machine no unnecessary parts. This requires not that the writer make all his sentences short, or that he avoid all detail and treat his subjects only in outline, but that every word tell.*

  — William Strunk Jr (*Elements of Style*)

- *The most valuable of all talents is that of never using two words when one will do.*

  — Thomas Jefferson

- *A multitude of words is no proof of a prudent mind.*

  — Thales

NOTE

If you have split a long article into separate sections, you should also consider providing your readers with a separate, printer-friendly page containing the whole item. These complete documents can also be presented within a single archive.

Start here

If only! As well as creating our smaller, logically organized sections, we require to make allowances for the fact that,

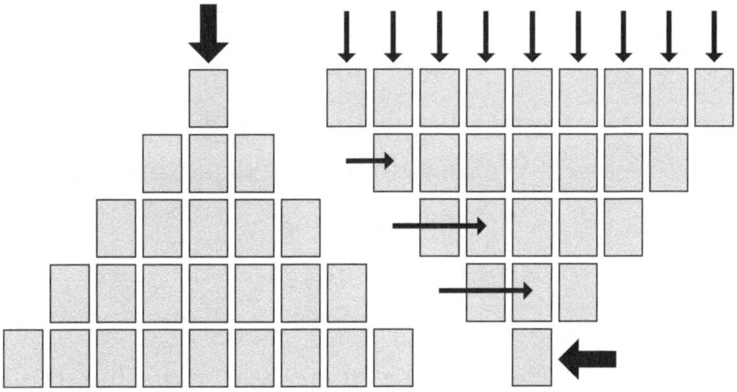

[Fig. 1.0]
Web readers don't always enter by your home page and then drill down. They can enter the site through many doorways.

on the Web, readers can enter content by way of **many paths**, particularly if they have followed a search engine link (Fig. 1.0).

Therefore, each section should, where possible, be capable of standing alone, effectively acting as an **individual doorway** into the site. Clear **explanatory headings** and useful **introductory paragraphs** help this to be achieved.

Article summaries are also extremely useful. According to the Stanford-Poynter reading news on the Web study (http://www.poynterextra.org/et/i.htm), most readers (nearly 80 per cent) read article summaries rather than complete articles.

In addition, **pointers** and **links** to other sections will help readers to navigate throughout the rest of the relevant content.

As an example of section organization, a series of articles I created on the subject of Internet Marketing included the following items:

- Introduction to Internet Marketing
- Search Engine Optimization

- Search Engine Pay Per Click
- Email Marketing overview
- Email Marketing creatives
- Email Marketing deployment
- Viral marketing
- Link building
- Internet advertising banners and buttons.

Of course, there were more but the key was that each could be independently consumed – rather like a set of related but individual fact sheets.

The same approach can be taken to individual sections which have depth. For example, Search Engine Optimization might further break down to:

- Overview
- Keyword research
- Title tags
- Keywords
- Descriptions
- Optimization of textual content
- Site structure
- Links.

Get to the point – pyramid style

In time, this should become an instinctive writing approach for you. As it happens, it is also another rule which is common to the Web and good newspaper content. That is, to:

- start the story with the **conclusion**
- follow with the most important **information**
- end with the **background**.

And, when creating your introductory material (the lead statement), the other key newspaper rule should be at the forefront of your mind:

- Who?
- What?
- When?
- Where?
- Why?
- How?

As earlier discussed, the majority of newspaper articles begin by answering most of these questions.

EXAMPLE

From the *Daily Mirror*:

A £1BILLION drop in mortgage lending suggests the house price boom could be starting to slow.

Borrowing dipped from £24.8billion in April to £23.8billion last month.

The Council for Mortgage Lenders said sky-high prices and rising interest rates were putting the brakes on the market.

Crucially, it added that the drop in lending was driven by a fall in the number of people taking out a mortgage to buy a house.

Separate figures from the British Bankers Association showed May had the smallest monthly rise in mortgage advances since November last year.

Lending by major banks rose by £4.9billion, well down on the record £6.4billion increase in April.

Bank of England governor Mervyn King issued a stark warning last week about the outlook for house prices, suggesting a fall was more likely.

A senior economist said yesterday: 'Maybe the message is starting to get through. But one swallow doesn't make a summer.'

The Building Societies Association said: 'People should be sensible about the amount they borrow as house prices are likely to rise less rapidly.'

This is known as the **inverted pyramid** style of writing.

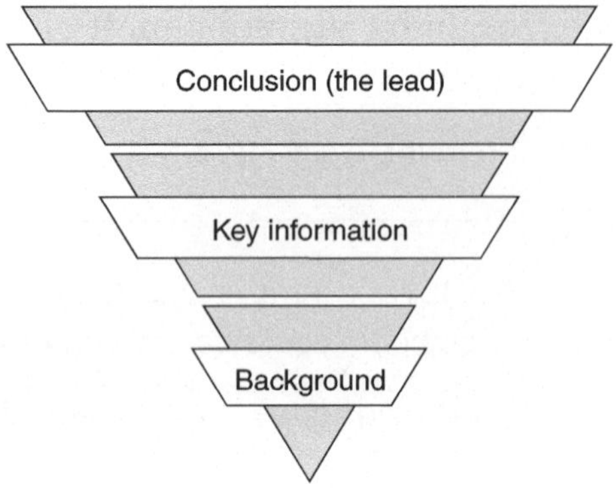

The effectiveness of the inverted pyramid style of writing on the Web is because the reader (the one who skims, scans and skips) can **quickly consume the key information at the beginning** (yes, the lead statement – the first two-to-three paragraphs) without necessarily reading the whole article.

This, of course, is opposite to the approach that is often taken, for example, with academic work, which is usually written in the more traditional pyramid style with conclusions coming last.

However, while it may not come naturally to some at first, it is the most effective way of approaching copywriting for the online readership.

NOTE

It can sometimes be difficult to create the conclusion before you have written the whole piece. Therefore, all you have to do is write your material as you would naturally and, when the conclusion becomes apparent, move it to the beginning.

The beginning is the most important part of the work.
— Plato

If you start with a bang, you won't end with a whimper.
— T.S. Eliot

In addition, since your readers can only see one screen at a time, the pyramid approach allows chunks of related information to be included within short, viewable sections of perhaps three to five paragraphs.

Bite the bullets

While you may have some difficulty imagining the usage of **bullets, points** or **sub-headings** in the works of Shakespeare or Dickens, they are essential elements to **grabbing** and **holding** the attention of the online reader and assisting their navigation.

And it's that **attention** that matters most in the first place, otherwise any actions you seek – or readers' goals sought – will not have a happy conclusion.

- Headings
- Sub-headings
- Bullets and other typographic devices
- **Emphasis**
- *Highlighting*
- Links.

They all help the skimming readers to find the key elements of your copy without reading complete articles.

Accessibility

The approach described above will also make your content more accessible to people with disabilities. For example, usability testing by The Communication Technologies Branch of the United States National Cancer Institute found that most blind users are just as impatient as most sighted users.

They want to get the information they need **as quickly as possible**. When using a screen-reader, they do not listen to every word on the page – just as sighted users do not read every word.

They '**scan with their ears**', listening to just enough to decide whether to listen further.

They listen to the first few words of a link or line of text. If it does not seem relevant, they move quickly to the next link, next line, next heading or next paragraph. Where a sighted user might find a keyword by scanning over the entire page, a blind user may not hear that keyword if it is not at the beginning of a link or a line of text.

Therefore, the guidelines are as follows:

- Write for the web.
- Write in short, clear, straightforward sentences.
- Use bulleted lists.
- Put the main point at the beginning of a paragraph.
- Write links that start with keywords.

And, in its **Top 10 Guidelines for UK local government websites**, the Cabinet Office (e-Government Unit) says:

- Text should be in plain language.
- Text should be short, scannable, broken up by unambiguous (rather than clever) sub-heads, and by bullet-point lists.

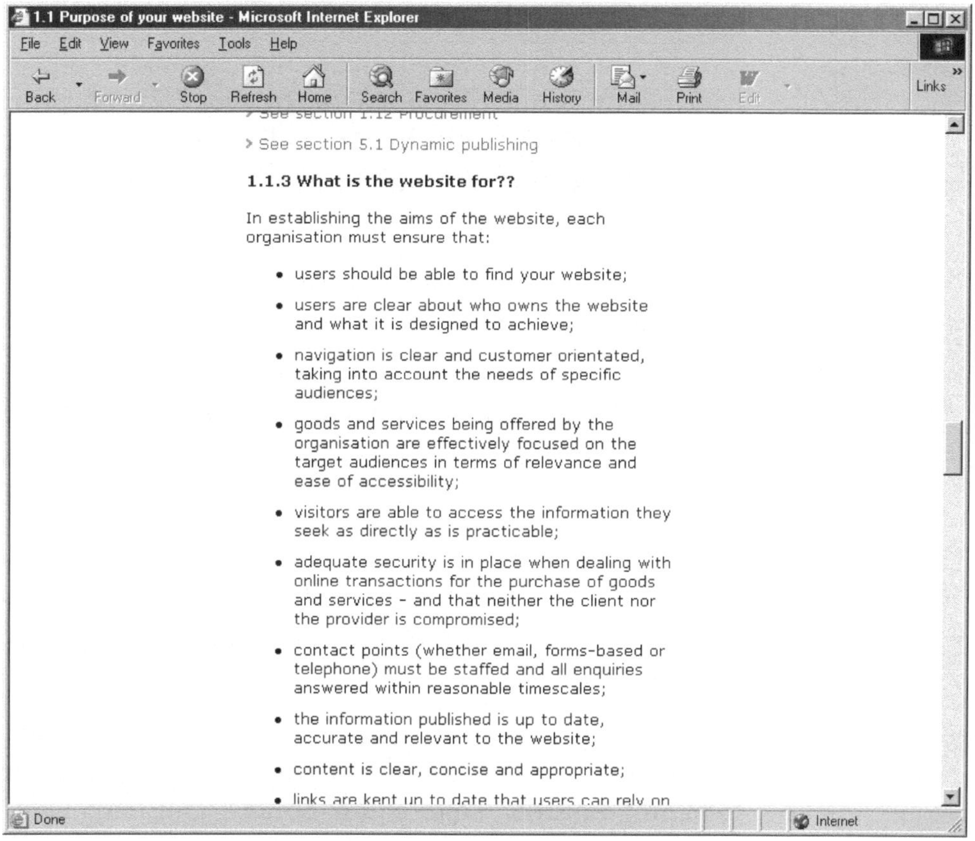

[Fig. 1.1]
The Cabinet Office (e-Government Unit) – practising what they preach.
http://www.cabinetoffice.gov.uk/e-government/webguidelines/

- Upper levels of the website should quickly make clear to users what is on offer and whether it is relevant to them.
- Lower down in the site, text and design should aim to communicate main messages and explain services simply and quickly.

In other words, you will create the most effective online content if you '**accessify**' **it for all**!

Interactivity

Interactivity is one of the key differences between print and online, whether it be **hypertext links** or the **opening of a dialogue** between reader and author through email or forms.

As a writer, you can enrich the reader's experience by, for example, providing links to external or additional related content.

You can also **elicit feedback** which can perhaps be used to influence future content – allowing the reader to become a more active participant in the process.

This participation can be given a sense of immediacy through, for example, **polls** related to your content and even live discussion or newsgroup-style **message boards**.

With or without your own participation, these discussion areas can bring a completely different form of life to your content. Forget the 'Letter to the Editor'. Your initial writing can be the catalyst for **lengthy discussion** and **contributions** from readers across the globe, putting them squarely into the action.

In addition, your writing for email or the Web can feature **strong interactivity**, by encouraging responses and entering into a dialogue with your readers.

On email, it is important to note that your writing very often takes a **one-to-one** form of communication rather than a broadcast to an audience and, in these cases, it should be particularly designed to motivate that person to act.

Alternatively, the interactivity sought may be more **viral-related**, to encourage people to encourage others by passing the email to their friends and associates.

The one-to-one relationship

As mentioned above, a one-to-one style of writing should often be adopted when writing for email.

However, this approach of **speaking 'with' readers** as opposed to 'at' them is extremely effective in all forms of online content creation.

A colleague more accustomed to financial numbers rather than written words, once asked me how to write.

My answer? '**Speak the words as you write them.**'

If it makes sense when speaking to yourself, it should be equally clear to your reader. Of course, you don't have to speak out loud – or you just might be taken away, my friend!

And, while your writings may be read by thousands of people, if you keep 'talking' to that **one reader** in a fluent manner you will have gone a long way to engaging **each of them** individually.

Also by engaging them in a **conversational style** you can draw them more easily to your main objectives and develop a personality they can relate to.

Summary

Once you've mastered the art of copywriting for online, the style and approach will come naturally. Indeed, the structured approach along with adding elements of style along the way should also enhance your enjoyment, self-organization and productivity when writing.

Checklist – copywriting for online

[ ] Can my key content be quickly and easily consumed?

[ ] Is the most important information at the start of my copy?

[ ] Have I enhanced the readers' experience?

[ ] Will my copy keep readers engaged?

[ ] Have I written in such a way as to gain the desired actions?

[ ] Will my copy deliver the objectives?

[ ] Have I answered the questions Who, What, When, Where, Why, How?

[ ] Have I included article summaries?

[ ] Have I organized content in an easy-to-follow and intuitive structure?

[ ] Is my material broken up into shorter-than-print, logically organized sections?

[ ] Have I started articles with the conclusion, followed by the most important information and ended with the background (inverted pyramid style)?

[ ] Is each of my sections capable of standing alone?

[ ] Have I used pointers and links to assist navigation between sections?

[ ] Are my sentences kept to about 15–25 words?

[ ] Have I used one idea per sentence?

[ ] Are my paragraphs kept to no more than four sentences and, preferably, two?

[ ] Do my paragraphs only contain sentences that relate to each other?

[ ] Have I used logical transitions between paragraphs?

[ ] Have I effectively used headings, sub-headings, bullets, **emphasis** and *highlighting*?

[ ] Is my content likely to assist accessibility?

[ ] Have I used plain language?

[ ] Do my introductory sections make it clear what is on offer?

[ ] Does my other material describe, explain and inform simply and quickly?

[ ] Have I provided separate single-page articles for printing purposes?

[ ] Have I used elements encouraging interactivity?

[ ] Have I used a one-to-one, conversational style of writing?

Have something to say, and say it as clearly as you can. That is the only secret.

— Matthew Arnold

CHAPTER 2

The Fundamentals

Overview

There is a fundamental approach to online copywriting that works. If followed, your reader will feel much more connected with you and trust the content you have created.

That's a sure way to create a **happy reader** and convert them into an **active customer**.

Chapter objectives

The content of this chapter is intended as a guide against which you can ask yourself if you have adhered to the fundamentals of online copywriting. **Every item** you create can be assessed against this.

If you feel your words don't quite match up, then start again. Because, if you think the text is not quite right, your readers will feel the same.

Chapter structure

- Know your reader
- Reveal your personality
- Build credibility
- Humour – it only hurts when they don't laugh
- Promotional writing
- Persuasion
- Summary
- Checklist.

Know your reader

As said in this book's introduction, its **main aim** is to help you to:

- say the **right** thing,
- in the **right** way,
- to the **right** person.

So, before you start copywriting for online, it is very important to establish **who** you are writing for and **why**.

For example:

- What are the readers' **expectations/goals**?
- Is your reader a business person or a consumer?
- There may be more than one core reader type. Identify them but try to keep it to no more than three to five.
- Perhaps give them names, roles and/or company positions that fit their profile – create their personae.
- What do they know already?
- What tone and style of language do they use?
- What phrases do they use?
- What do you seek or expect from them?
- What do you want to give them?
- What is the purpose (the overall objective) of the material you are writing?
- Are there any sub-objectives?

TIP

It can also be useful to create a sentence or two summing up what you are trying to achieve and for whom.

On **creating personae**, as well as giving names and roles or company positions to your target readers, you can find images that look like them, print them off and have them looking back at you as you write and edit!

For example, an image search on Google (http://images.google.co.uk/) for 'businessman', led me to a choice of different types of people (suited, busy, young, middle-aged, etc).

One result can be seen in Fig. 2.1 – a middle-aged, well-dressed, polished and relaxed-looking executive.

He might fit the profile of one of my typical readers if I was, for example, writing about investments.

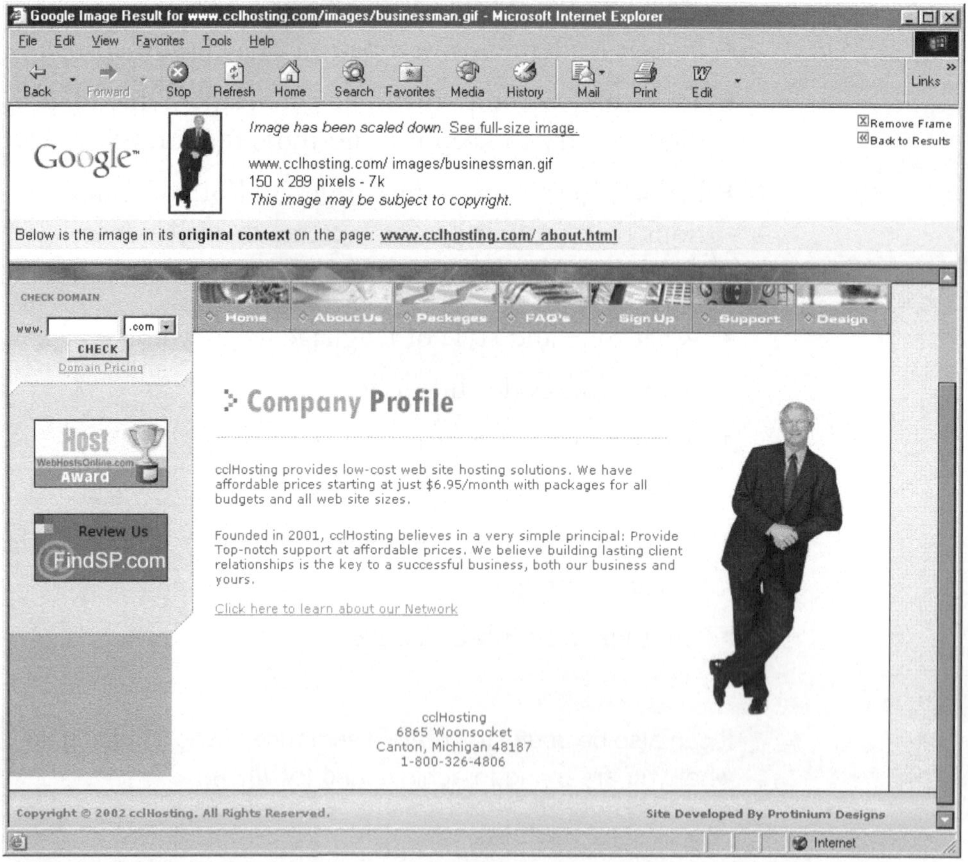

[Fig. 2.1]
One result of a Google images search for 'businessman' – my man Michael.

My persona for him might be:

- Name: Michael
- Age: 52
- Position: Company Director
- Main Goal: To gain a 50 per cent profit from an investment within five years
- Financial status: Funds available for investment
- Knowledge of subject: Medium to high
- Most likely to be persuaded by:
  - — Clear information which emphasizes the benefits he would gain by making an investment
  - — Supporting facts and figures
  - — Comparison charts
  - — Testimonials from similar people
  - — Company history and credentials.

NOTE

It's very important to bear in mind that the **key goals matter most** when creating a cast of personae. If you know what your readers want to gain from your content – or the goal you want them to adopt as their own – you will more successfully identify the correct personae.

Of course, my character, Michael, would not be the only persona relevant to my project. It's possible I would see him as my main persona and that I would also develop other secondary personae (perhaps three to five) and endeavour to satisfy their needs, too.

Once you have worked through this process – effectively endeavoured to become your customers – it will be much easier for you to write the correct content for the target readership and not just any Tom, Dick or Harry!

Reveal your personality

A great deal of online content is bland and uninteresting – words simply poured in to fill the space left by designers.

However, websites and email that **convey personality** give the readers a sense of a real person beyond the screen.

As a result, they will **stay longer, read more** and **respond more readily**.

That doesn't mean every item of content has to begin 'Hi, I'm David and welcome to my little place on the web . . .'.

Rather, you create a **voice** and **tone** to present a consistent **style** the target readership will relate to and remember.

The voice is created through your choice of words as well as how they and the sentences are structured (complexity, length, active or passive, etc).

The tone is created through your attitude towards the subject matter and your reader (chatty, formal, casual, authoritative, etc).

EXAMPLE

Here is the review of the movie *The Day After Tomorrow* from FHM.com:

Bugger around with Mother Nature and she'll screw you right back. That's the message, and when man's abuse of the planet backfires it sparks disaster. There's tidal waves, twisters and snowstorms a plenty in this effects-strewn behemoth.

As the next Ice Age takes hold we follow one man's rather pointless attempt to rescue his son – stranded in the frozen Big Apple . . .

The pixel-picture CG set-pieces are frankly, astounding. Just as well, because there's a huge dollop of cheese to sit through as Jack Hall (Dennis Quaid) straps on his snow shoes and heads off to save his son (Gyllenhaal), who's sat burning the New York public library in a bid to stay alive.

And here is the same site's intro to its SkinCare column:

Face glowing redder than a baboon's arse? Plagued by acne or simply just wondering what moisturiser to use? Then it's a good job skincare expert Amanda Banks is here to give you answers to all your problems . . ..

'Bugger around with Mother Nature . . .', '. . . there's a huge dollop of cheese . . .', '. . . redder than a baboon's arse . . . ?' You wouldn't have that on your corporate site but this is the voice, tone and style of a lads' mag and it clearly works for them.

http://www.fhm.com

Simply, the style, tone and voice all have to do with how a piece of writing **sounds to the reader** and what **impression it makes**.

Through your use of a voice, tone and style, the readers will also, in their mind's eye, build a picture of the site owner. The readers experience and the way you communicate to them should be like a **personal meeting** with that owner/publisher.

With regard to a business website, the voice, style and tone will also convey a sense of the values of the company, encouraging readers to become customers. That is, of course, if your material is also presented in an effective manner for your online readership.

[Fig. 2.2]
FHM.com speaks the language of its laddish readers.

EXAMPLE

Here is how ICS Learn at one time introduced their offerings:

Take a distance learning course and broaden your horizons! Whether you're looking for vocational training, business studies, academic qualifications or even just to start a new hobby, we provide a wide range of distance learning courses covering a wide range of topics.

ICS has been the world's number one in home study for over a hundred years, helping people just like you achieve their goals. Designed for maximum flexibility, distance learning courses are ideal for anyone who needs to study at their own pace. Browse our Course Catalogue, select the course you want and buy online today. Home study with ICS – the better way to a better job, better future . . . and a better life!

This was positive and active and, to an extent, put the reader into the action. However, as you can see in Fig. 2.3, the two chunky paragraphs didn't score too well on the scannability front. And a sampling in the 'We We'* test (see below) produced a Customer Focus Rate of 50 per cent.

Therefore, ICS Learn's offering was replaced with the text below.

Take a distance learning course and **broaden your horizons** with the World's Number One in home study! We have over 200 courses for you to choose from.

You can study at **your own pace**, with the reassurance of **total support** from **highly trained** staff every step of the way, whether you choose:

> Vocational Training
> Business Studies
> Academic Qualifications
> A new hobby

You are just three simple steps away:

1 **Browse** the course catalogue

2 **Select** the course you want

3 **Start** learning today

Home study with ICS – the **better way** for you to have a **better job**, **better future** . . . and a **better life**!

You **can do it**!

Chattier, active and much more scannable, with the benefits and actions clear to be seen (see also Fig. 2.4). Which means it was more likely to be read. Which means it was more likely to convert readers into customers! Plus it produced a Customer Focus Rate of 82 per cent.

http://www.icslearn.co.uk

*For the '**We We**' test, see:

http://www.futurenowinc.com/wewe.htm

And Chapter 5 – Writing For Websites.

One way you can establish the correct personality is to use language that would be correct for **someone you know** who fits the profile of your intended audience.

And, from a corporate perspective, it's important to develop or adhere to the '**brand voice**'. This is the written part of the brand identity, which should be consistent across all material created for customer consumption.

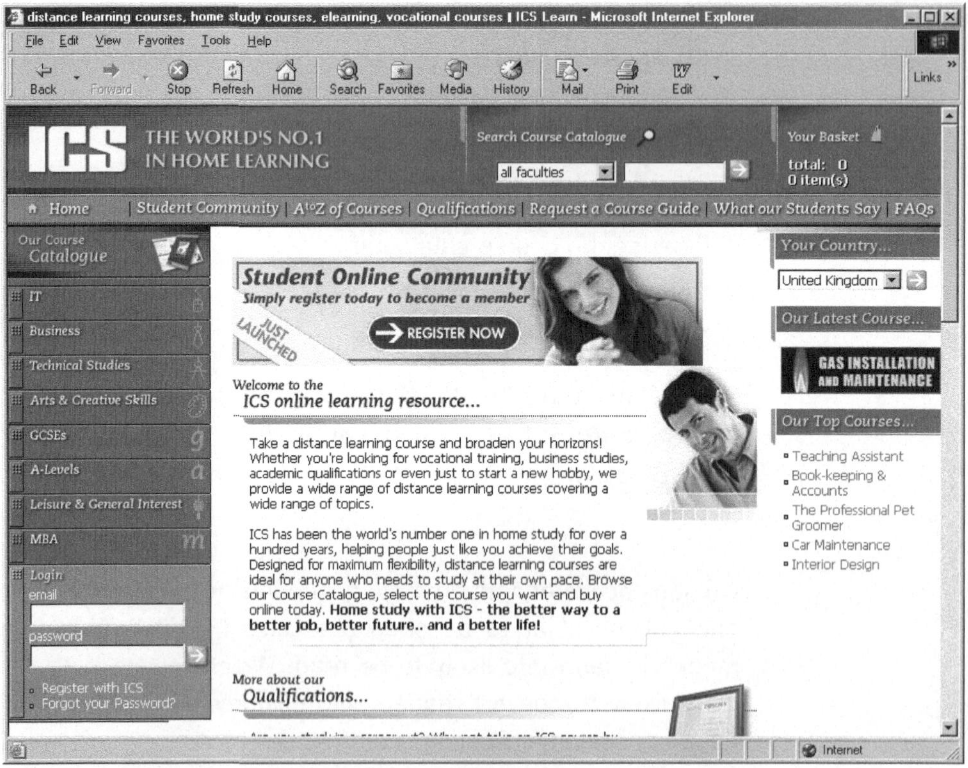

[Fig. 2.3]
ICS Learn (before).

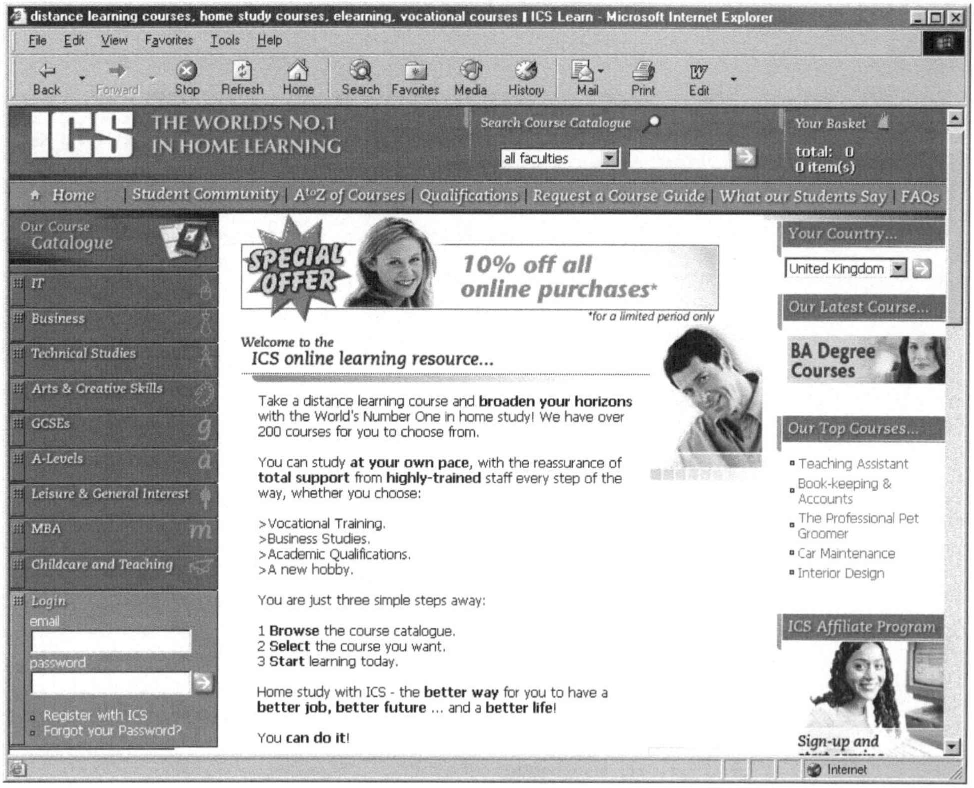

[Fig 2.4]
ICS Learn (after).

Again, **writing as you speak** in a more informal style will strongly influence the personality you convey and help gain the confidence of your reader.

> TIP
>
> Your **personality** should be modified so you use a style of language your typical readers will understand and relate to. It is based on what they are like. For example, you would adopt a different kind of personality if your audience was a group of teenagers rather than a collection of industry leaders.
>
> Your **tone** should be modified so it fits the role you wish to play. For example, are you a tutor, a fellow professional or a good friend?

Build trust and credibility

Through the successful development of the personality you convey, and the quality of content published, you will also score more highly on the trust and credibility front.

Credibility is a **key factor** if you are to gain the confidence and trust of your reader.

Credible content is:

- Well-written
- Interesting
- Useful
- Objective
- Personable
- Up to date
- Accurate
- Easy to navigate.

NOTE

A survey carried out by the University of California, Los Angeles (UCLA), found that only 53 per cent of users believed most or all of what they read online.

Humour – it only hurts when they don't laugh

Unless you are a comedian or the publisher of a jokes database, humour requires to be used with caution.

No matter the time you will have spent getting to know your reader, they may well have already heard 'the one about . . .' or the humour falls flat.

However, a little humour can go a long way, particularly when used to develop your personality. And it can help bring some life to an otherwise fairly dry subject.

So, it's best to remember it's not only the **way** you tell it, it's also about **who** you tell it to!

NOTE

Humour on Topic

If you are introducing humour, as well as making sure it suits your readership, don't forget to make it on-topic.

In this context, I might have written *'Did you hear the one about the copywriter who . . .'

Alternatively, one might have penned '**BABES AND HUNKS!** Okay, now I have your attention . . .'

The latter may well have stopped you momentarily but it would be completely off-topic and would more likely turn you away than raise a smile.

*If you **have** heard 'the one about the copywriter who . . .', I'd love to hear it, too:-)

Email: david@writingediting.co.uk

Promotional writing

Ah, here it comes . . .

1. Why this book is the ideal guide for **marketers** wishing to write and edit effective online content.
2. The secret to **successful promotional hype** and marketese.

Well, **yes**, to the former and **no** to the latter.

Because, when it comes to the web, promotional writing is **significantly less effective** than text which is:

- Objective
- Informative
- Punchy.

That is what sells and wins over readers.

And this goes back to **credibility** and **trust**. If a reader hesitates to question if a promotional claim is accurate, it slows them down. Their questioning can also damage credibility.

The greatest snake oil you can buy

Really? Am I to believe that? Don't think so!

10 simple reasons ProductX will benefit you and why

Okay, tell me objectively, honestly and accurately.

Offline direct mail marketing material is often littered with extravagant adverbs and adjectives. 'Greatest', 'Best', 'Leading', etc. Online, it's the facts you present that require to speak for themselves.

Jargon, as well as unfamiliar acronyms and abbreviations, should also be avoided unless you are writing technical content for a knowledgeable readership.

Any acronyms and abbreviations that you do use should be defined in the first place unless they are readily understood by your typical reader. For example, CID is okay but you would use SEO (Search Engine Optimization).

Try to use words that are **familiar** and **frequently used** by your readers. If you must use terms which may be unfamiliar to some of your readers, it would be helpful to provide a glossary also.

And it's quite possible that people from other countries, those having English as a second language, will be readers, too. This is another reason why you should use simple, easily understandable language.

> **TIP**
>
> One way to find your readers' frequently used words is to assess which search terms are being used on search engines to find your relevant products, services or information. This information is often revealed by web analytics packages.
>
> Overture's Term Suggestion Tool is also helpful. It can be accessed in the Advertiser Centre at:
>
> http://www.uk.overture.com
>
> For example, when I entered 'email marketing', I found the second most-used search phrase was 'direct email marketing'.
>
> You can also assess words used in a within-site search facility.

On the jargon front, you might also like to try Bullfighter™. This is software that runs in Microsoft Word and PowerPoint, within Microsoft Windows 2000 or XP. It works a lot like the spelling and grammar checker in those applications, but focuses on jargon and readability.

As Deloitte Consulting, the people behind Bullfighter™, say:

'Stripping the Bull Out of Business.'

'A value-added, leverageable global knowledge repository.'

'Repurposeable, leading edge thoughtware that delivers results-driven value.'

'A future-proof asset that seamlessly empowers your mission critical enterprise communications.'

'Bullfighter™ could be all of these things. Except that we have no idea what any of these things are!'

Bullfighter™, is available from:

http://www.deloitte.com

Blocks of text in CAPITAL LETTERS, should be avoided, too. THIS IS MUCH MORE DIFFICULT TO READ than if I'd written it 'this way in lower case'.

And, when you're writing your own material or editing that of others, make sure you **consistently call a spade a spade** (rather than at certain points referring to it as a shovel!).

Otherwise, your reader will become confused about the item, begin to have doubts and, quite likely, hop off to find another site.

Persuasion

Last in this chapter but not least . . . persuasion. Particularly from a marketer's perspective, there is one desired outcome – that the **reader takes action**.

And the aim of your content is to persuade them to do so.

All of the elements described above will make your material more persuasive and the key factor is gaining the readers' **trust and confidence**.

The stronger your credibility, the more likely you are to provoke your **desired actions**.

Of course, brand plays a large part in building confidence. I would be confident in financial information provided by the Royal Bank of Scotland. But a newly created .com financial portal would have to work harder to persuade me of their credibility.

And they (and you) would do that by persuading me:

- they know me
- they know what I need and want

- they can provide me with what I need and want
- they have anticipated and answered my questions and doubts
- they offer real benefits.

And, through this persuasion –

- I can trust and have confidence in them.

Summary

By building a clear picture of who you are writing for, you will be able to strike the ideal tone and style for your target readership. Credibility will be built through good, accurate content, especially if jargon and marketese are avoided.

These are among the fundamentals of writing and editing online. And, also, don't forget to follow one of the **principles of marketing copy** – **KISS** (Keep It Simple, Stupid)!

Checklist – the fundamentals

[ ] Do I know my reader?

[ ] Is it a business person or a consumer?

[ ] Is there more than one type of core reader?

[ ] Have I given them names or company positions to fit their profile?

[ ] Have I identified their key expectations and goals?

[ ] Do I know what they know already?

[ ] Have I used the correct tone and style of language?

[ ] Do I know what I seek or expect from my readers?

[ ] Have I written as I speak?

[ ] Will my material be seen as being credible?

[ ] Have I put the readers in the action?

[ ] Is the content interesting?

[ ] Is the content useful?

[ ] Is the content objective?

[ ] Is the content personable?

[ ] Is the content up to date?

[ ] Is the content accurate?

[ ] Is the content punchy?

[ ] Are the benefits and actions clear?

[ ] If I've used humour is it correct for the readership and on-topic?

[ ] Have I avoided the use of hype and marketese?

[ ] Have I avoided the use of jargon?

[ ] Are unfamiliar acronyms and abbreviations avoided or kept to a minimum?

[ ] Have I defined any acronyms and abbreviations that have been used?

[ ] Did I identify my readers' familiar and frequently used words and phrases?

[ ] Have I used their familiar and frequently used words and phrases?

[ ] Have I avoided the excessive use of capitals?

[ ] Have I persuaded my reader to take action?

What is written without effort is read without pleasure.

— Samuel Johnson

CHAPTER 3

Sub-editing – Tuning Your Copy

Overview

Accurate ... easy to consume ... scannable ... concise. Common themes keep arising regarding the creation and presentation of effective content for the online readership. Good sub-editing is a key factor if we are to consistently achieve our goals.

Chapter objectives

This chapter covers some of the basic rules related to sub-editing and preparing your copy for publication online. It will help you to look at your material with an objective eye – particularly by considering the rules related to good sub-editing – and lead to the presentation of consistently well-tuned copy.

Chapter structure

- Introduction
- Editing your own copy
- Headings and sub-headings
- Hyperlinks
- Setting the styles
- Summary
- Checklist.

Introduction

In his introduction to *The Simple Subs Book,* the aforementioned Leslie Sellers wrote:

Let's first establish what subbing is about. A sub is required:

- to ensure that everything checkable has been checked – and that goes for names, places, titles, dates and anything else that could possibly be wrong
- to make sure that the story as subbed is **intelligible, easy to read** and **appetising.**

Later, he writes that: [the sub-editor's] 'news sense must be the reader's news sense, professionally sharpened. He has to be able to pick out the dominant fact, or the talking point, and put it **right there at the top** so there is no danger of the customer missing it.'

Thus, subbed text should be the following:

- Accurate
- Easy to read
- Appetising
- With key content at the top.

While written in 1968 from a newspaper perspective, these are still **golden rules** today with regard to writing and editing online.

Editing your own copy (and that of others)

In the days before direct input, I used to feel some sympathy – just a little – for the news reporters when their cherished copy was screwed up into a ball by the Chief Sub and thrown 'down the table' to be rewritten.

In actual fact, it's not a sub-editor's job to rewrite every piece of copy that lands on their desk. If it's not broken it doesn't have to be fixed!

And you and I don't have to conduct major surgery on every item we create either. That is just as well because editing your own copy can be an equally difficult task.

However, whether it's our own copy of material created by others, we can take a step back and endeavour to look at it from a **reader's perspective**.

- Is it accurate?
- Is it the correct length (remembering that less is more)?
- Is the key information at the start?
- Is it easy to consume?
- Is it scannable?

When we can confidently answer 'yes', the job is done.

TIP

A Fresh Eye

When possible, do try to get at least one other person to check over content. Again in the old newspaper days, we would take five paper proofs of pages to be read by different people. In most cases, **each person had a valid change** that hadn't been added by another.

Also, even though the copy is intended to be read online, print it out for checking if you can. More mistakes are missed when reading on screen, which is probably why an increasing number of errors appear to be creeping into online and print material these days.

As a sobering thought and also for some lighter relief, here are some gaffes I encountered that have previously made it into print:

We apologise for the error in the last edition, in which we stated that '[Mr Fred Bloggs] is a defective in the police force.' This was a typographical error. We meant of course that [Mr Bloggs] is a detective in the police farce.

A transplant surgeon has called for a ban on 'kidneys-for-ale' operations.

Sister Gillian's 'bust clinic' referred to last month was, of course, a 'busy clinic'.

The all-girl orchestra were rather weak in the bras section.

FOOTBALL BONANANZA!

I recall the last one was printed in 180pt type.

Of course, when material appears online, it is usually much easier to have any errors changed after they've been published either directly or as a result of a word in the ear of a friendly web developer. But, by then, the **embarrassment factor** may have already kicked in.

Headings and sub-headings

A key way to make your copy more scannable is to use headings and sub-headings.

They will **increase interaction** and **conversions**. For example, a longish amount of apparently bland text about distance learning courses may well be consumed and, eventually, the reader just might click here.

But more people would convert if it was broken up with:

Distance Learning – The Benefits

Why Book Online

How To Book Online

Start Your Degree Here

It does seem rather obvious, but all too often the writer's craft and the sub-editor's key contributions are being lost online to designers and developers who simply fill holes with what they see as grey matter (aka written content, to us).

Headings and sub-headings should also be **meaningful** to help the reader understand what is coming next. Of course, in many cases, they will pass some by and focus on the section of content which has the heading **most relevant** to their interest.

Due to the fact your readers see one screen at a time, it's also better to use more headings than you would normally include for print.

In addition, sub-headings can increase interactivity when used as extra calls to action:

Find Out More About Distance Learning

And they can be used to further convey personality:

Ok, here's my distance learning nitty gritty

Sit up class! The finer points you need to know

Psst – my secret to gaining full marks

Great – now let's complete the booking form

Plus, for variety, you might like to use thematic newspaper-style **crossheads** to break up sections of text:

LEARNING

STUDYING

WRITING

COMMUNICATING

PASSING

Any of the above methods will:

- make your copy more scannable
- help guide readers through the content
- make the material appear more appealing to the eye
- capture your readers' attention.

So, have fun with headings and sub-headings and make them work for you and your readers.

NOTE

I've even known sub-headings with one initial uppercase character used to spell out a message. For example:

Your courses

Outline of options

Understand distance learning

Preparing for exams

Assessment of progress

Studying later

Secret to success

The message: **YOU PASS**

But don't be tempted to follow the example of the disgruntled staff copywriter who used the characters to spell out something rather unpleasant about his boss. He was quickly seeking alternative employment!

Hyperlinks

Hyperlinks will also attract your readers' attention. Therefore, as well as being meaningful, it's best if they are included at the end of sentences (where we expect the conclusion to be).

For example:

The section on Writing for Search Engines will help you understand the importance of key phrases, titles and descriptions.

Would be better as:

To gain a better understanding of the importance of key phrases, titles and descriptions, visit the section on Writing for Search Engines.

This also helps to avoid breaking up the sentence – a link mid-sentence distracts the reader and can hinder their comprehension of its content.

In some cases, you may alternatively wish to have the link at the start of a paragraph. In these circumstances, the text that follows should be additional descriptive information.

For example:

- About Writing for Search Engines – the importance of key phrases, titles and descriptions.

In addition, by being meaningful, links will tell the readers what they're going to get if they click, effectively as if they were a title. This is also important so readers can choose **not to click**. It's hard enough to retain attention so why encourage unnecessary hops from page to page?

This is also true of general navigation links. How often do we see:

- Next
- Back
- Top
- More

This would be better, for example, as:

- Next: House style
- Back: Headings and sub-headings
- Top: Sub-editing introduction
- More: Hyperlinks in practice

Further, good links do not need to be signalled. 'Click here to . . .', 'Follow this link to . . .' etc. Your reader knows what a hyperlink looks like and what will happen when they click on it. It's making the content of the link meaningful that matters most.

Setting the styles

'When interpolating explanatory material, please use square brackets.'

I've no idea why, but that one-sentence memo has doggedly refused to leave my memory banks since I first read it in the offices of the Hobart Mercury, in Australia, many years ago.

Maybe it's because I disagreed. 'He [Joe Bloggs] claimed to . . .' I'm sorry, but while this might have been correct, it just didn't work for me [the tabloid journalist!]. 'Joe Bloggs claimed to . . .' would have been my style.

However, it didn't matter whether I agreed or not because that was the **house style** and following it was an **absolute requirement**.

House style is essential if you are to maintain **uniformity** and **consistency** in your writing.

Another example is the publisher of this book requiring the use of single quotes for ordinary quotations and double quotes within single quotes for a quotation within a quotation.

To me [that tabloid newspaper man again], that's the wrong way around. But, once more, it's the set style.

Many organizations have their own set styles and, as in the examples above, the key rule is that they should be **followed consistently**.

I Say email, You Say E-Mail! I Say Website, You Say Web Site. Let's **not** call the whole thing off, Mr Astaire! If no styles exist, you should have **your own set**.

- Are you a single or double quoter?
- Colons, or colons and dashes?
- Commas or spaces in big numbers?
- Bullets with full stops or semicolons?
- Are your dates 1st April or 1 April?

In addition, it can be useful to draw up a list of commonly used terms to achieve consistency. For example, do you refer to people on your site as 'users', 'readers', 'guests' or 'visitors'?

You may have a small list to begin with but this should be added to as you generate more content and review material produced by others.

House style

While you may wish to create your own house style or already have one in existence, here, for reference and as a starter for 10, is one provided by the publishers of this book,

Butterworth-Heinemann, for the purposes of manuscript preparation:

Spelling

Butterworth-Heinemann's house style is to use -ize endings when optional. Note, however, that the following words should always be spelt -ise:

advertise	disfranchise	misprise
advise	disguise	mortise
affranchise	emprise	practise (verb)
apprise (inform)	enfranchise	precise
arise	enterprise	premise
braise	excise	prise (open)
chastise	exercise	reprise
circumcise	expertise	revise
comprise	franchise	seise (legal term)
compromise	guise	supervise
concise	improvise	surmise
demise	incise	surprise
despise	merchandise	televise
devise	misadvise	treatise

The following should be spelt -yse, not -yze (except in American spelling):

analyse	dialyse	hydrolyse
catalyse	electrolyse	paralyse

Follow *The Collins English Dictionary* for spellings and word breaks.
Follow *Butterworths Medical Dictionary* for medical spellings.

Punctuation

Commas: Use them where they are essential to the sense.

Colons: A colon usually introduces a list of items. Never use a colon and dash together as the colon alone is adequate.

Quotes: Use single quotes for ordinary quotations and double quotes within single quotes for a quotation inside a quotation.

Hyphens: Follow *The Collins English Dictionary* for hyphenation. The trend is toward reduced use of the hyphen (e.g. trade-off, mainframe, textbook). Retain hyphens, however, between double vowels (e.g. re-establish) and where required to convey a particular sense (e.g. re-sign rather than resign, three-day-old chicks rather than three day-old chicks).

Note the use of hyphens in compounds (e.g. long-term plans) and with 'well' and 'ill' (e.g. a well-produced book). Insert hyphens in compounds where the same consonants end and begin the constituent parts (e.g. cold-drawn, cross-section).

Dashes: The typesetter will set a spaced en rule for dashes. The en rule is slightly longer than a hyphen. An unspaced en rule is used to connect specially related names and properties (e.g. the Adams–Harris equation, stress–strain ratio). The unspaced en rule is also used to denote a span of numbers (e.g. pp. 5–15).

Abbreviations: House style is to include full points after abbreviations but not after contractions (in which the shortened form ends with the final letter of the word).

Thus: Eq., Fig., Prof. (for Equation, Figure, Professor) but Dr, Mr, Ltd (for Doctor, Mister, Limited). Plurals (e.g. Eqs, Figs) take no full points.

Stops are required in such abbreviations as etc., e.g., i.e., and c. (circa) which use lower case letters.

Stops are not required where upper case letters are used as in the initials of an organization (e.g. BBC, UNESCO) or abbreviated scientific terms (e.g. DNA, GMO). Do not begin a sentence with an abbreviation.

Numbers

In general works, spell out numbers under 100. In technical and scientific writing only numbers below 10 should be spelt out unless they are accompanied by units.

Where numbers larger and smaller than 100 are mixed use figures for both.

Always spell out a number which begins a sentence.

Four-digit numbers should be closed up with no space or comma (e.g. 5000, 3725, etc.) unless they are in tables and have to range with other longer numbers. Numbers of five digits or more should be divided by a space between three-digit groups on either side of the decimal point (e.g. 28 673.826 1).

Decimals should generally be used in preference to fractions. Decimals below unity should carry a zero before the decimal point (e.g. 0.63 not .63). Decimal points are set on the line. Where fractions are essential use a solidus in running text (e.g. 1/2). Where fractions are displayed a two-line fraction can be used. The solidus should always be used for complex fractional indices so that they can be printed on one line (e.g. $2 \times {}^{(m + n)}/_{3}$).

The term billion should be either avoided or explained. The term has different meanings in the UK and the USA.

Use the shortest unambiguous form for ranges of numbers (e.g. 16–17, 23–4).

Do not use Roman numerals [except where essential for a third level with a list after 1, 2, 3 and (a), (b), (c)]. They are less easy to comprehend and in listings give a ragged effect.

Always use a numeral with the term 'per cent' (e.g. 15 per cent).

Capitalization

Keep capitalization to a minimum. Too many capitals tend to be typographically ugly on the printed page.

Use initial capitals for proper names, official titles, trade names and specific features in the book itself (e.g. Figure 1.1, Chapter 3).

Proprietary drug names, when used, have an initial capital [e.g. diazepam (Valium)].

Italics

Italics slow the reader down because they are less easy to read than ordinary type. Use them sparingly in the text.

Only unanglicized words and phrases should be italicized, not foreign words which have become familiar through constant use (e.g. via, et al., in situ, are not italicized).

Use italics for book titles and periodicals, films, operas, plays, names of ships and microbiological nomenclature where strict species terminology is used.

Units

SI units should be used exclusively.

Any departure from SI units should be discussed with your commissioning editor. If 'old' units have to be used the SI equivalent should usually follow in parentheses.

Symbols

Figures should always be used with units (e.g. 10 mm) and there should always be a space between the figure and the unit (e.g. 10 mm × 10 mm = 100 mm).

The preferred style for partial pressures is as follows: Po_2, Pao_2, Pco_2 etc.

A distinction should be made between a symbol for a physical quantity and a symbol for a unit. The former is set in italic (e.g. electromotive force, *E*), whereas the latter is set in ordinary type (e.g. volt, V).

Italicization of superiors and inferiors follows the same rules as for other symbols. Unit symbols are always in the singular (e.g. 25 kg not 25 kgs).

Equations

If mathematical and chemical equations are used, number them per chapter. The numbers should be ranged right. Display where possible with a line of space above and below:

$$2(a - b - c) = (a - b - c) + (a - b - c)$$

If an equation is long and the line turns, break at =,+, or −.

Ratios

There should be no space either side of a colon indicating a ratio (e.g. 1:7).

Brackets

Where several brackets have to be used in a mathematical expression the sequence should be [[⟨{[(. . .)]}⟩]].

Vectors

Vectors should be set in bold type.

Miscellaneous

Per cent: Spell out per cent as two words in literary contexts, but in statistical contexts and in tables and diagrams where space is scarce the symbol (%) is acceptable.

Proprietary names: Proprietary names such as Terylene, Vaseline and Perspex require an initial upper case letter.

Dating: Avoid vague phrases that may date your book (e.g. 'in the past decade', 'will soon be introduced'). It is better to replace these with specific dates. Avoid quoting specific prices of goods and services – if you must include them indicate the year to which you refer.

Dates: Use the form 15 August 1999 (not 15th August 1999). Do not use numerals – 7.6.99 means 6 July 1999 in the USA.

Do not put apostrophes in decade spans (use 1950s not 1950's).

Do not use the expressions 'thirties' or 'eighties', etc. but 1930s, 1980s, etc.
Use 'from 1958 to 1959' not 'from 1958–9'.

Spell out the names of centuries (e.g. 'the eighteenth century' not 'the 18th century').

PS from me:

On the web, avoid the use of <u>underlines</u> – they will most likely be mistaken for hyperlinks.

And, for the UK readership, I would always use -ise endings when optional.

Plus, yes, I'd prefer the use of double quotes for ordinary quotations and single quotes within double quotes for a quotation within a quotation.

But that's my kind of style!

TIP

The Name Game

Be very careful with names. There is nothing worse than misspelling the name of a person, organization or product. From the website of *The Guardian**:

'When I see my name spelt with one word, I want to slap and choke people. If you do that, you got to be a moron. It's on every poster, every album and every ticket as two words. If you spell it as one, you're an idiot. Bottom line.'

Meat Loaf

**The Guardian* was the first newspaper to publish its style guide on the web. It can be accessed here:

http://www.guardian.co.uk/styleguide/

Does it matter to your reader? Absolutely. This is more than simply good practice – the use of consistent styles **makes your content easier to consume**. In addition, it conveys the impression of one person speaking – that *personality* again – rather than multiple personalities saying things in different ways.

And as Charlie Morris – formerly managing editor of *The Web Developer's Journal* – wrote in 1999: 'A writer who submits work that is error-free and in the proper style stands out like a pearl of great price.'

I wish!

Summary

To give Mr Sellers his place once more, he wrote: '**The good sub can write clearly, crisply and concisely**.'

I would add that's also true of the good online writer.

Checklist – sub-editing

- [ ] Is my content: Accurate?
- [ ] Is my content: Easy to consume?
- [ ] Is my content: Scannable?
- [ ] Is my content: Concise?
- [ ] Is my content: Intelligible?
- [ ] Is my content: Appetising?
- [ ] Have I checked everything that is checkable?
- [ ] Is the key content at the top?
- [ ] Have I written/edited to the correct length?
- [ ] Has at least one other person proof-read my material?
- [ ] Have I printed out and read the copy on paper?
- [ ] Have I used useful headings and sub-headings?
- [ ] Have I used links effectively?
- [ ] Do my headings and sub-headings include calls-to-action?
- [ ] Do my headings and sub-headings convey personality?
- [ ] Have I used consistent house style?

Reading maketh a full man, conference a ready man, and writing an exact man.

— Sir Francis Bacon

CHAPTER 4

Website Content Planning

Overview

If you are writing the material of a new website, the first thing you should prepare is a Content Plan. Not only will this ensure you cover your subject appropriately, it will result in a **logical navigational structure** for implementation by the site developers.

Chapter objectives

The purpose of this chapter is to help you create a content plan which will reflect the **categories**, **sections** and **sub-sections** of your web writing project. The methodology will also allow you to identify relevant existing and to-be-created content as well as assist the prioritizing of tasks.

Chapter structure

- Introduction
- Structure
- Contents
- Frequency and Forward Planning
- Summary
- Checklist.

Introduction

In Chapter 1, we covered the creation of smaller, logically organized sections and the need to make allowances for the fact that, on the web, readers can enter content by way of many paths.

If they are to be useful, websites also require to be easy to navigate.

Your content plan will go a long way to ensuring all of this is successfully achieved.

Structure

The first thing to do is make a list of the likely **structure of the site** (the information architecture – IA). For example, for a smaller site, I might have:

- Home
- About Us
- Our Products/Services
- FAQs
- Privacy Policy
- Contact Details.

NOTE

A key consideration is to establish a **goal/purpose for each page** – particularly the value/usefulness it delivers to your readers. To this end, it's useful to begin by creating a list of goals and then ensuring each has a page within the final structure. For example, one list of goals might include:

- Describe the benefits delivered by Products X, Y and Z.
- Help the reader identify a local reseller.

- Answer questions about Service A.
- Explain the ordering process.
- Illustrate ease of use.

This approach will also help the website to gain better search engine positioning as topic-focused pages score more highly when relevancy is assessed.

I would then make a list of any likely sub-sections. For example, Our Products/Services might have the following sub-sections:

- For the Home
- For Business.

And they might have further sub-sections.

As well as describing the content as a textual list, it is also often helpful to have a **visual representation** in the form of a tree diagram. This can be created in Word, Excel or PowerPoint or, for a more elaborate schematic, Microsoft Visio is an excellent tool.

Figure 4.1 shows how the above site structure would look as a tree diagram.

On a larger project, your lists and tree diagram will also reveal the complexities of the website. While you may not think your role is to be the site architect, you do want your content to be **easily accessible** and **well organized**.

Therefore, you should adjust the structure (adding/ removing/modifying/moving sections and sub-sections) in a way that seems most logical.

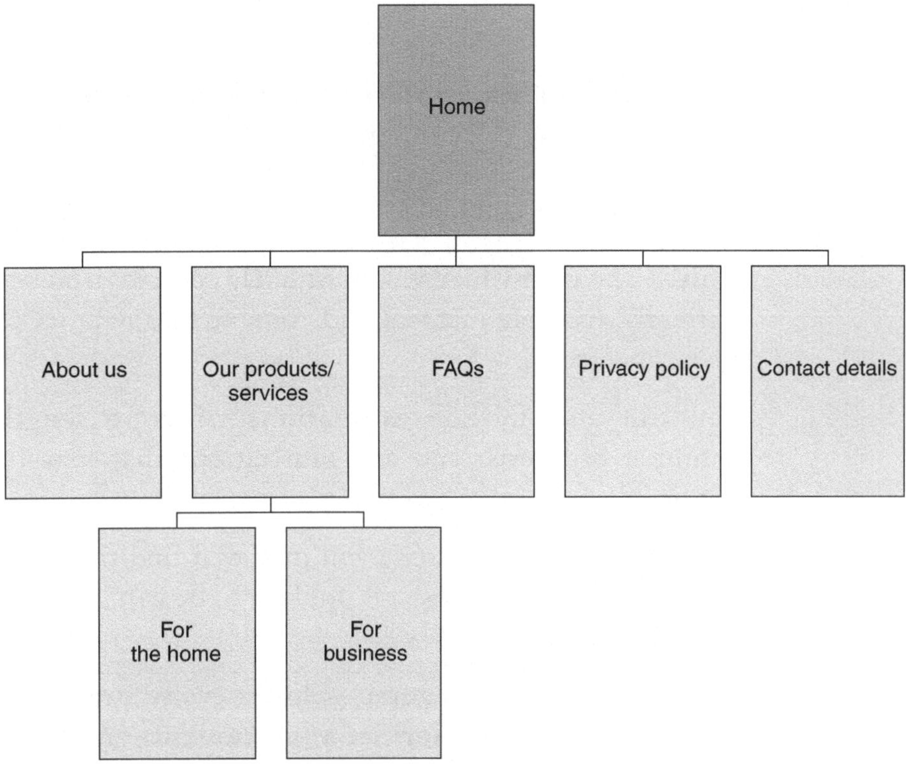

[Fig. 4.1]
Tree diagram of a small website.

For example, do you have an all-encompassing section called **Fruit** or do you have a Fruit section with sub-sections for **Oranges** and **Apples**?

Time should also be spent on identifying the names of the sections and sub-sections.

- Will they make sense to your reader?
- Do they effectively label their intended contents?

As described by Webmonkey (http://hotwired.lycos.com/webmonkey/), information architecture is the science of figuring out what you want your site to do and then constructing a blueprint before you dive in and put the thing together.

Contents

Once you have defined the structure of the site, you can begin **describing the contents**.

- What items should be presented within each section?

This is a new list which will most likely contain details of currently available material and content that requires to be newly created.

You can also include **estimations of copy length** (number of words) and any illustrations that may be applicable.

By conducting this exercise you may well find that your lists are so long the website is unlikely to be completed in the next 5 years!

Fortunately, by their nature, websites evolve over time. Therefore, you can **prioritize your contents** and break your lists into phases.

For example, you might have:

Products Overview > **Product Category Description** > **Product Details**

But, for Phase One, you could choose not to have the **Product Details**.

Frequency and forward planning

In most cases, the launching of a website is not an ending – it's a beginning.

Whether the content is about widgets or world wonders, the site owner becomes a publisher and, with your help, should have a strategy to **add**, **update**, **modify** and **change**

prominence of material as required to consistently meet the initially identified objectives.

At the outset, it's advisable to draw up an outline on how this is to be achieved. For example:

- Draw up a calendar of relevant events or milestones which would trigger a need for new content or a change of emphasis.
- Create a procedure that ensures all new press releases or products/service descriptions are published.
- Have a general schedule for regular updates and adhere to it.

If there are multiple authors or external sources of information, you can also endeavour to become the site editor. In this case, you'd:

- co-ordinate the collection of material
- proactively pursue it
- generally manage all content online
- liaise as required with development staff.

With regard to the editor role and depending on the volume of content, you might also consider employing a Content Management System (CMS) to automatically set publication and expiry dates and generally ease the production flow and content updating processes.

Summary

A well-constructed content plan will help you to produce the ideal copy for your online project. It will also satisfy the needs of your reader and, most likely, gain you many new friends within the web development arena.

Checklist – website content planning

[ ] Have I accurately described the structure of the site?

[ ] Are all required elements included?

[ ] Is the structure simple and logical?

[ ] Are the sub-sections effectively organized?

[ ] Have I given the sections and sub-sections names which will make sense to my readers?

[ ] Do the names I've given effectively label their intended contents?

[ ] Have I established a goal/purpose for each page?

[ ] Have I listed the correct content for each area?

[ ] Have I created a visual tree diagram?

[ ] Have I identified the source of existing, reusable material?

[ ] Does my list reveal items which require to be newly created?

[ ] Have I estimated copy length for each item?

[ ] Are any applicable illustrations listed?

[ ] Is my workload prioritized?

[ ] Have I created a plan for different phases?

[ ] Have I created a forwarding-looking editorial plan?

Good plans shape good decisions. That's why good planning helps to make elusive dreams come true.

—Lester R. Bittel

CHAPTER 5

Writing for Websites

Overview

Okay. We know all about skimming and scanning, personality, credibility, editing and style. But here's the real test: putting it into practice while, at the same time, adapting our approach for different purposes and various audiences.

Chapter objectives

The bulk of the contents of this book will help you to create effective content for websites. However, this chapter focuses on some specifics which will make your writing **relevant** and **useful** to whatever target market you are trying to reach or influence.

It will also reinforce the message that, no matter how good the design, it's **the words that really matter**.

Chapter structure

- Introduction
- The Science
- Home Pages
- Destination Pages
- About Us
- Privacy
- Summary
- Checklist.

Introduction

As online copywriters we require to be extremely adaptable if we are to successfully:

- say the right thing
- in the right way
- to the right person
- to achieve the **right results**.

However, by following a certain methodology and asking ourselves key questions we can consistently write content which works for a diverse range of websites.

The science

Before you begin writing, it is essential to have a game plan.

What are the goals? To:

- increase sales?
- gain leads?
- provide information?
- elicit feedback?
- prompt registrations?
- provide support?
- build brand awareness?

In addition:

- What is the target audience?
- What do they want?
- How can you best meet their expectations?

Yes, lots of questions. But, if you ask and answer them **before you start writing**, you will be well prepared to produce content that is effective for your readers and your paymaster. In other words, you have to think like your customer/reader.

Next, you have to become an expert in the subject matter. Products, services, information. . .

- What **makes it different**?
- What are the **main benefits** it can deliver to your readers?
- Are there **secondary benefits**?
- Why is it **better** then offered elsewhere (or how can it be presented to appear better)?
- Are there **features** and **specifications** that require to be detailed?

On the last point, it's easy to assume your readers know more than they actually do. While it's important not to dumb-down the content, your readers might well have questions or problems which you must **anticipate, answer** and **solve**.

In general:

- Give answers before explanations.
- Give summaries before details.
- Give conclusions before discussions.

If possible, seek out typical readers/customers and ask them some questions about their **expectations**, **knowledge** and **needs**.

Also examine your competitors' sites, identify what they do well and then **do better**!

This is the science – the often painstaking detective work – that takes the risk factor out of the creativity that is to follow.

Home pages

Quick – you have 10 seconds to grab my attention, draw me to the products, services or information I'm seeking and lead me into the site!

That is the two 'A's of the **AIDAS** test – grabbing **Attention** and encouraging **Action**. And that's the main purpose of any Home Page, no matter the audience or subject matter.

The reader has arrived with expectations that they require to be fulfilled in a timely fashion.

As in the Science, above, a useful approach is to again put yourself into the action:

- I'm a customer.
- I know what I want.
- Is it there before my eyes?
- Can I click to get it?

Or:

- I know the kind of thing I'm seeking.
- Is this site likely to fulfil my need?
- Can it quickly lead me to satisfaction?

And don't forget there are many Doubting Thomases out there:

- I don't believe you.
- I don't need it.
- I don't have enough time.
- I can't afford it.
- It won't work for me.

So, it's important to **anticipate any objections** and provide answers for them.

Of course, the reader will be **scanning**. To put this into some perspective, consider the illustration that follows (Fig. 5.1).

[Fig. 5.1]

PS: Inspired by Gary Larson's excellent cartoon in *The Far Side* series. (http://www. thefarside.com)

The human character says: 'If you don't stop chewing up my clothes, there will be no more doggy treats or nice walkies outside! Do you understand!!!'

The dog hears: 'Blah, blah, blah, blah, blah, blah, blah, blah, blah, blah, blah, **DOGGY TREATS**, blah, **WALKIES OUTSIDE**, blah, blah, blah . . .'

In that case, the dog heard the only words it knew and the rest was just noise. But web readers also try to filter our peripheral information and focus on **content, benefits** and **calls to action** that are pertinent to them.

Within a web page content like this . . .

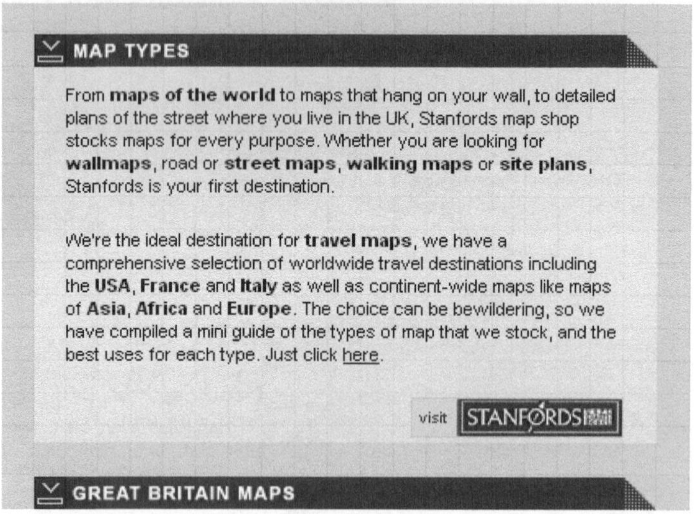

[Fig. 5.2]

. . . the scanning reader would focus on:

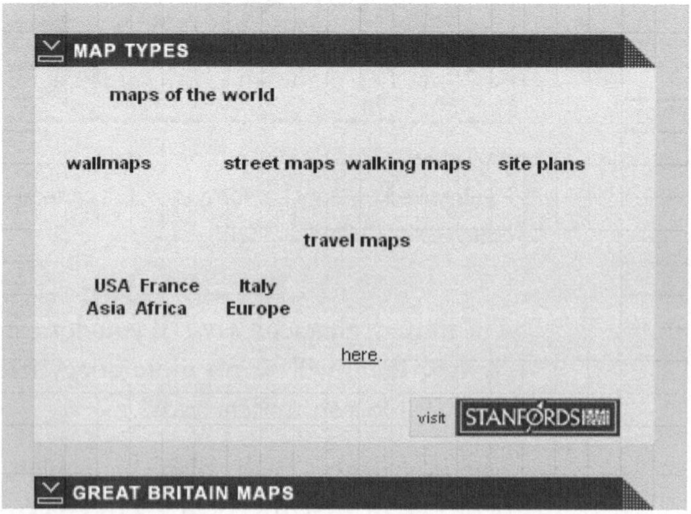

[Fig. 5.3]

In addition, the Home Page content will be more promotional in tone. That doesn't mean it features 'marketing hype'.

Rather, it **actively**, **clearly** and **objectively** presents 'what's inside the packet', helping the readers reach the ingredients of their choice and immediately see the benefits available to them.

Your voice for the Home Page (and the rest) should be as **active** as possible.

- **Active Voice** is a sentence style in which the subject performs the action.
- **Passive Voice** is a sentence style in which the action is performed on the subject.

'A does B' is much more effective than the passive 'B is done by A'. In addition, the active voice tends to be more customer-centric than the passive and it helps to speed up your readers' understanding.

For example, the active:

MediaCo generates high search engine positioning.

Is better than the passive:

High search engine positioning can be achieved by MediaCo.

Other advantages of the active voice include:

- Sentences are usually shorter.
- The communication style is more direct.
- Actions are brought to life.
- Strong verbs help the reader know who is acting and what is being acted upon.
- The content is less ambiguous than the passive voice.

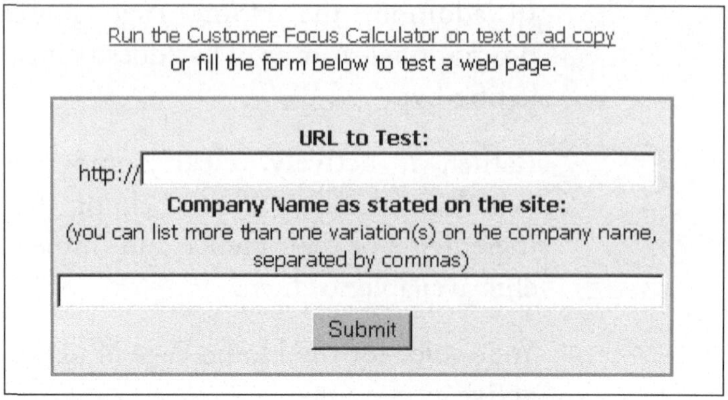

[Fig. 5.4]
Future now's 'We We' calculator.

With regard to being customer-centric, you must also endeavour to pass the so-called **'We We' test**. That is, putting the reader rather than yourself into the action.

And, if you're unsure whether your copy will pass the test, you can try Future Now's free 'We We' customer focus calculator at:

http://www.futurenowinc.com/wewe.htm

> **TIP** When possible, begin paragraphs by describing benefits. And get to the point quickly before the scanning reader moves on.

All your pages should also contain **positive content**. For example, if I were to write 'the web server is not idle', the reader would most likely **slow down** and convert this text into the positive 'the web server is running', which is what I should have written in the first place.

Indeed, anything that slows the reader and hinders the flow of comprehension is a strong negative. Therefore, you should try to maintain your **positive waves** throughout your writing.

Destination pages

Having used the Home Page to guide your readers to the source of their interest, the other key pages – the **Destination Pages** – are where you 'deliver the goods'.

Knowledge, products, services . . . ; whatever the focus, the content should continue to be **useful, informative** and **credible**.

And, while it is still important to be as succinct as possible, scrolling and deeper content is more acceptable on destination pages.

Also, by this time, you will have anticipated the needs and goals of your readers and identified the **depth and breadth** of content that is necessary to deliver satisfaction. This, for example, might include the following:

- Comparisons
- Examples
- Service descriptions
- Product tours
- How-to guides
- Walk-throughs
- Fact sheets
- White papers
- Case studies.

So, through this process, you can have short, sharp and focused top-level pages (summaries and conclusions) supported by as **much content** as is required without ever being concerned about providing either too much or not enough.

Beware, however, about expecting your readers to drill down through multiple levels. This is because they are, eventually, likely to **feel lost in the depth of the site** and may even have followed a path to content that doesn't, in fact, meet their expectations.

It is **better to offer breadth** – meaningful links to content which is one step away from the upper levels and, when possible, also directly accessible from each sub-level.

In addition, if you have ever become lost while walking around an unfamiliar town, you will appreciate the value of a local map with that big **'You Are Here'** arrow.

This is also particularly true on the Web, when readers reach content either as a result of jumping from section to section or entering a website by way of an external link.

Therefore, each section and page within it should show the readers **where they are located** within the bigger picture.

One way of doing this within your copy is to include **'breadcrumb trails'** at the top of your articles.

For example:

Home > Products > ProductX > Description

Not only will this assist your readers, the site developers will thank you. And they will (or should) either use the text-based breadcrumbs within the pages or create graphical signposts instead.

Every site of any substance should also feature a **Site Map**, listing the full contents in a logical fashion (home, top sections, related lower pages, etc.).

This should be accessible from all pages and provides readers with a **one-click-away** route to any page as well as offering an overview of the site as a whole.

Once again, you can help your readers, help boost search engine positioning AND make your content more accessible by providing **meaningful link content**.

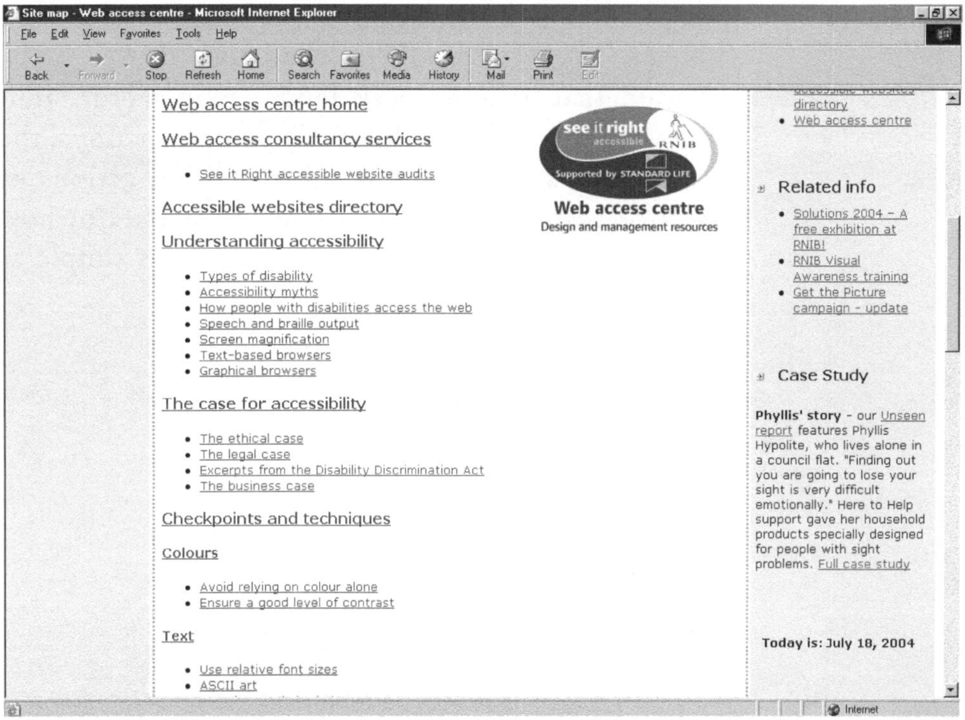

[Fig. 5.5]
A site map published by the Royal National Institute of the Blind (RNIB).

A good example of a useful text-based site map is published by the Royal National Institute of the Blind (RNIB) – http://www.rnib.org.uk – within its Web Access section (Fig. 5.5).

Instructions

When your content contains **instructions**, tell your readers **what to do** as opposed to what to avoid doing.

For example, 'Read the Product Fact File to find the most suitable model' is better than 'To avoid ordering the wrong model, read the Product Fact File.'

Actions

It is said that actions speak louder than words. But, when your words fail to effectively describe actions, the only **action is inaction**! So, when writing actions or tasks (for example, how to download software or how to identify the correct product), make it as simple as ABC.

For example:

- Step 1
  Do this . . .
- Step 2
  Do this . . .

EXAMPLE

The Royal Navy's instructions regarding the downloading of wallpaper images (Fig. 5.6):

Downloads – Wallpaper – Instructions

How to set images as your wallpaper.

Please remember: Navy News and Navy News Online grants permission to use these images ONLY as wallpaper and they are not for general distribution.

Windows (Internet Explorer and Netscape)

1 Select the dimensions of the picture most appropriate to your screen resolution.
2 Open the picture and right click on the image.
3 Choose 'Set as Wallpaper' from the menu that appears.

Macintosh system 8.0 and above

1 Select the dimension of the picture to download for your screen resolution. If in doubt, select the largest picture as

your Macintosh will adjust the size of the image to fit your desktop.

2 Click on the link to that image and hold down the mouse button. Select 'Download Link to Disk' (Explorer) or 'Save Link As' (Netscape). This will download the picture to your computer. Remember where you save it!

3 Open the 'Appearance' control panel and click on the 'desktop' tab. Then drag the newly downloaded picture onto the image of the screen.

4 Click on the 'Set Desktop' button and close the control panel.

---

http://www.navynews.co.uk/downloads/instructions.asp

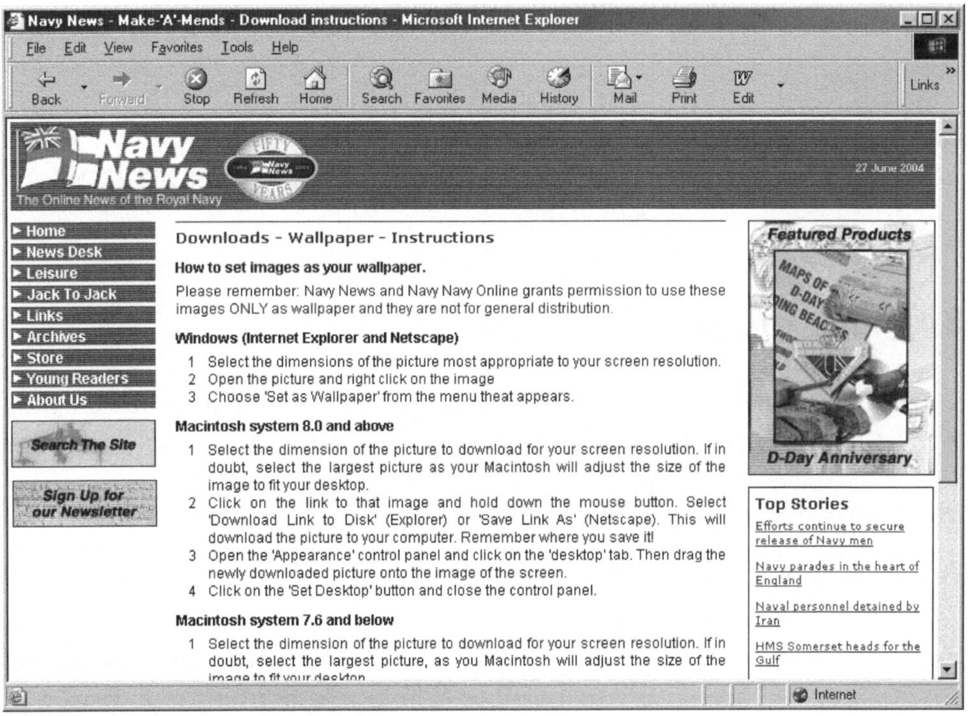

[Fig. 5.6]
Download instructions from the Royal Navy.

NOTE

It's easy – but wrong – to assume your reader will know what to do next when faced with a possible action. Therefore, you should always anticipate they may need some help and that explanations and instructions should be provided within the text or as a separate file.

In addition, when you are requesting information from the reader, perhaps within a form, tell them why you need it.

For example, if I am asking a reader for the name of their favourite pet, it's because 'it will increase their security and will be used for identification purposes in the future' rather than being some sort of nosiness on my part.

You may also be required to write the content for forms. If so, forget the Census and keep it as simple as possible – the more you ask of the readers, the more likely they'll stop and go elsewhere.

TIP

As a rule of thumb, while the page length of a Home Page should be no more than twice the screen height (perhaps 200 to 300 words to a screen), Destination Pages can be up to four screen heights.

Scoring the goals

Having identified the aims of your activity, you can then modify your content accordingly. So, here are some scenarios . . .

Increasing sales to *the Shopper*

In this case you want to hit the spot as quickly and as effectively as possible. The initial content that is viewed by the Shopper requires to be short, sharp and powerful (but not pushy) . . .

- Emphasizing the benefits (but avoiding hype).
- Answering the questions.
- Removing the doubts.
- Revealing the value.
- Persuading them that you actually do have what they **need** and **want**.
- Motivating them to buy.
- Directing them where to go.

This should be supported by further more-persuasive information geared towards **solving their problems** or **satisfying their desires**. For example:

- Product/service details (the nuts and bolts and the **benefits** they offer).
- Uses and results (the product/service in action and the **benefits** gained).
- Comparison charts (why it's better and offers more **benefits**) – Fig. 5.7.
- Case studies and testimonials (illustrating the **benefits** enjoyed).

Benefits, benefits, benefits . . . yes, that's what sells and provokes actions! If you have described a **feature** and the reader says 'So what?', you've lost them. You, therefore, must always answer the question 'What's in it for me?'.

TIP

Psst . . . NEEDs and WANTs are different. For example, a potential buyer has reached your site because they 'need' a new PC. Why? Because the one they have, apparently keeps crashing. It's too slow. It's at least two years old!

But, guess what, they actually **want** a new PC to play the latest games, write DVDs and have a meaner machine than their next door neighbour does! So, if you can satisfy the **needs** and then **anticipate** as well as **effectively describe** how you will deliver the **wants**, then you're both a winner and a successful seller!

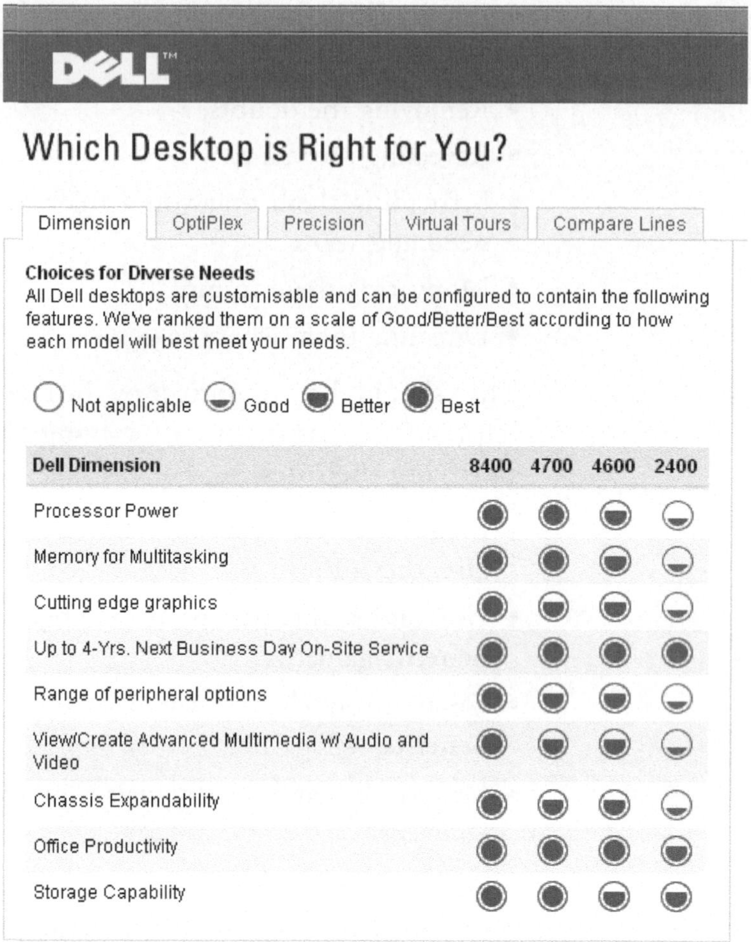

[Fig. 5.7]
Chart from Dell comparing its own range of Dimension desktops.

Also endeavour to strike a **friendly** and **helpful** tone. For example, think and be like your favourite shop assistant!

Generating leads from *the Browser*

If your aim is to generate leads, you are most likely writing to sell a product or service that people won't normally buy off the page.

Your prospect, the Browser, will be like a visitor to a high street shop who has entered initially to quietly **browse items** and **gain more knowledge** about them and the seller.

This reader doesn't want you to hit them with the hard sell or bully them to buy as soon as they enter.

Rather, they have visited your site – and, most likely, others, too – to help them to make an informed purchase at some point.

The factors that will make them choose your site to initiate contact include:

- ease of accessibility to value information
- quality of the information provided
- credibility of the information
- comparing the above with that presented by your competitors.

TIP

On credibility, the use of testimonials can be very beneficial; another's recommendation is stronger than any advertisement.

Providing information for *the Researcher*

The main mission of many sites is to provide access to useful information. Industry bodies, Government departments and health organizations are among the most active information providers.

In addition, many commercial organizations have informational sections within their sites or dedicated microsites that are intended to help readers make informed purchases.

To satisfy the Researcher, initial information should be short, sharp and quick to consume. For example:

- How to . . .
- Top 10 tips (Fig. 5.8) . . .
- Twenty things you need to know about . . .
- FAQs . . .
- The subject at a glance . . .

This can be supported with content of greater depth, downloadable files, etc.

Top 10 tips of all time

Top ten incredibly easy things that any fool can do to improve their health

1. **read a book or two** - now a prescribed treatment in some health authorities for beating the blues, reading in the evening also helps relaxation and sleep;
2. **open a window** - it lets in negative ions which neutralise the positive ions from electrical items;
3. **play cards and do crosswords** - keeps the brain active
4. **support a decent team** - success boosts testosterone levels which is why we're competitive. Identifying with a successful team can have the same effect.
5. **work on your relationships** - a study of 6,000 blokes found that the married ones got better jobs and were healthier.
6. **sleep long and get up late** - regularly getting 4 instead of 8 hours sleep brings forward the physical and mental signs of ageing. Late risers have faster brains and lower stress levels. Sleep well and live long.
7. **go out in the sun** - vitamin D, which is important for bones, teeth and happiness is boosted by sunlight (but keep the sunscreen on.)
8. **walk** - it's good for the heart and lungs and improves brain function by boosting its oxygen supply. Get off the bus a stop early. Take stairs not lift.
9. **sing** - the breathing control needed to sing - however badly - makes it one of the easiest and most effective ways to shed stress.
10. **drink water** - many of us don't drink enough. The yellower your urine the more dehydrated you are. A couple of extra glasses of water a day and you'll feel better.

NHS

The Department of Health has provided funding to the Men's Health Forum, assisting the provision of health information and advice.

[Fig 5.8]

Top 10 tips from the Men's Health Forum – http://www.malehealth.co.uk/

In this case, your readers will consume your content and come back for more if you successfully present material that is:

- Credible
- Authoritative
- Expert.

Holding on to *the Loyal Viewer*

Channel-hopping web readers can be very fickle and they are very particular about the sites they will bookmark and regularly revisit.

And most will also give serious consideration before becoming a registered subscriber, whether having to provide their precious personal details or make a payment.

If you are to first capture and then retain the Loyal Viewer, you must **recognize** and **consistently serve** them **what they like and want**.

And, if you take your foot off the pedal, they are likely to rapidly switch loyalties by going elsewhere.

So, factors that are important include the following:

- Value of content.
- Timeliness and relevance.
- Freshness of material.
- Interactivity (for example, through surveys, polls and forums) – Fig. 5.9.

Helping *the Solution Seeker*

Many online readers will arrive at your site with **questions** or **problems**. It is, therefore, important to try to

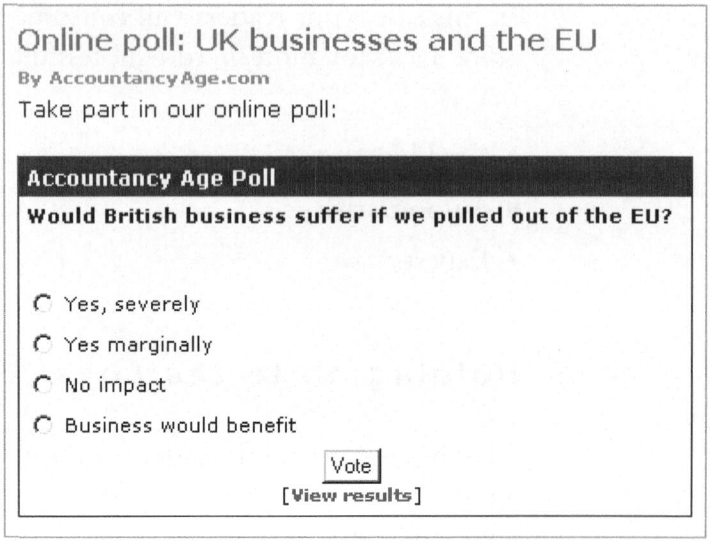

[Fig. 5.9]
Online Poll from Accountancy Age – http://www.accountancyage.com

anticipate these and lead the readers to the **answers** and **solutions**.

That is:

- Your question is . . .
- Your problem is . . .
- Here is the answer . . ..

Using logical assumptions, again putting yourself in the place of the reader, you can, for example, create a set of Frequently Asked Questions (FAQs) and answers – Fig. 5.10.

To build upon this and make it more useful, you should also ask for a reader response mechanism to be put in place.

In time, or immediately if the information is available, this can grow into a large Knowledge Base that could be browsed by topic or searched.

Frequently Asked Questions - FAQs

HMSO regularly receives questions about Crown copyright and other matters. Some of the questions which we are most frequently asked are set out below together with the answers. If there are any other questions which you think should be added, please let us know. You may also like to know that the Patent Office has produced a helpful booklet about copyright which can be obtained by telephoning 020 7596 6566 or e-mailing copyright@patent.gov.uk

To help you find the the answer to your query, we have split the questions into four sections:

- Crown Copyright
- Licensing re-use of Crown copyright material
- Official Publishing
- HMSO Website / Legislation Online

[Fig. 5.10]
FAQs from Her Majesty's Stationery Office (HMSO) – also split into sections.

The flip side of this is, if you do not **write clearly** and directly, with the needs of your audience in mind, your readers may be left with more questions than answers.

This can result in:

- misunderstandings,
- mistakes,
- complaints,
- increased enquiries,
- staff time lost to question answering and problem solving.

NOTE Don't forget the headings, sub-headings, bullets, etc!

It's not about you – it's About Us

Nearly every website you'll ever visit contains an **About Us** page. And, in most cases, suddenly the page author has forgotten to put the reader into the action.

'Okay, you've skimmed the first page so now you can read about **me, me, me** . . .'.

Wrong! The About Us page should be used to tell your readers **what you can do for them**.

Of course, it's still fine to introduce yourself and describe credentials, qualifications, key personnel, etc. But only if this helps to build your credibility in terms of the **benefits to the reader**.

Your privacy is important

Another key page is the one describing your **Privacy Policy**. If you are seeking to gather personal information from your readers (from email enquiry forms to online financial transactions), they need to trust you to keep it private (unless, of course, they actively give their permission – for example, by clicking a check box – to allow it to be used for other purposes).

The Organization for Economic Co-operation and Development (OECD) offers a free online **Privacy Policy Statement Generator** in co-operation with industry, privacy experts and consumer organizations.

The generator, which has been endorsed by the OECD's 30 member countries, including the UK, aims to offer guidance on compliance with privacy guidelines and to help organizations develop privacy policies and statements for display on their websites.

The generator can be accessed here:

http://cs3-hq.oecd.org/scripts/pwv3/Login.ASP

Whether using a policy generated in the above fashion or created through another means (for example, by your own legal department) you should edit it as required to make it:

- easy to read and understand;
- reflect the tone of your other content;
- put the reader into the action (what this means to 'you' rather than 'we do this, that or the other').

TIP

A good approach is to present your Privacy Policy in a form similar to that of Frequently Asked Questions.

For example:

- What do you do with my email address?
- Is the information I supply secure?
- Are my details shared with third parties?

You ask, we answer – FAQs

The 'You Ask, We Answer' page was a hugely popular feature in *The Weekly News*, a mass-seller when I joined it from school in 1977 to start my career in newspapers.

Some 20 years later, when I returned to the offices for a nostalgic visit, the circulation might have fallen somewhat but the same man was sitting in much the same area, doing much the same thing – opening letters containing readers' questions.

And while such as 'How to remove a coffee stain on my lace doily?' may be particular to *The Weekly News*, your **Frequently Asked Questions** (FAQs) page is likely to be a very well-read destination.

That is, if it successfully answers your **readers' most important questions**.

And to do so you should:

- **avoid listing too many questions**.
Split into logical groups or sections if required.

- **make sure you really do provide an answer**.
If the question was 'Can I find out how long my sentences should be?, it would be wrong to answer 'Information on sentence lengths can be found in Chapter 1'. The correct answer is 'Yes, in Chapter 1, it states you should try to keep sentences to about 15–25 words.'

- **avoid hype and marketese**.
When a reader sees a question about a product or service, they don't wish to be told in the answer that 'it's the best thing since sliced bread'. Rather, they want useful information most likely related to benefits and features.

- **make the questions clear**.
'What about email?' is vague. 'Can I generate email responses through the system?' is specific.

- **write the questions as 'I', the reader, would ask them in person**.
'Can I . . .', 'How do I . . .', etc.

- **avoid leading readers to a dead end**.
If the question was 'Can I gain technical support?' the wrong answer is 'Yes, you can visit the Help Section or contact customer support.' A correct answer is more like 'Yes, you can visit the *Help Section* [link] or contact customer support by email [insert email address] or telephone [insert phone number].'

- **put the readers in the action**.
'White wine is best kept chilled' would be better as 'You will taste the wine at its best if you keep it chilled in your fridge before opening.'

- **use a logical order.**

For example, use group-related questions or begin with the most commonly asked questions.

- **keep them updated.**

With the best will in the world, it is unlikely you will initially anticipate all of your readers' most important questions. So, encourage feedback and add to or modify your FAQs accordingly.

- **make sure the answers are accurate!**

If you're wrong, you will most likely lose your readers.

Help help

Going beyond FAQs, you may be required to create the content for more comprehensive Help sections containing a substantial amount of material.

Most often this be a mixture of FAQs and steps with instructions.

In the first place, you should, again, follow best-practice with regard to presenting and organizing the questions, particularly bearing in mind the reader's perspective and language.

Then, when instructions are required rather than straightforward answers, you should tell your readers what to do in as **few logical steps** as possible.

Each step should:

- be numbered;
- contain only one action;
- present clear instructions (and explanations as required).

(See Figs 5.11 and 5.12).

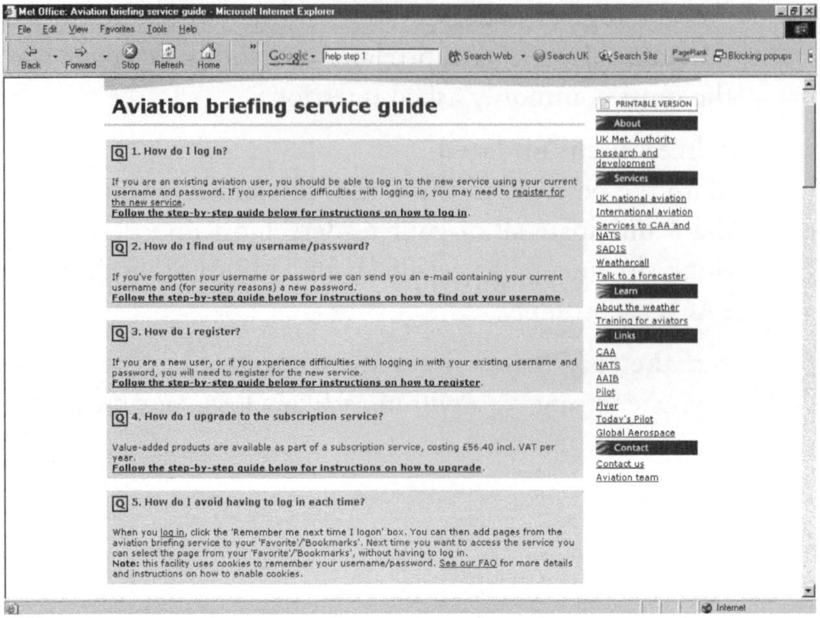

[Fig 5.11]

Within its Aviation Service help section, the Met Office (http://www.metoffice.com/) presents numbered questions followed by clear steps (Fig. 5.12).

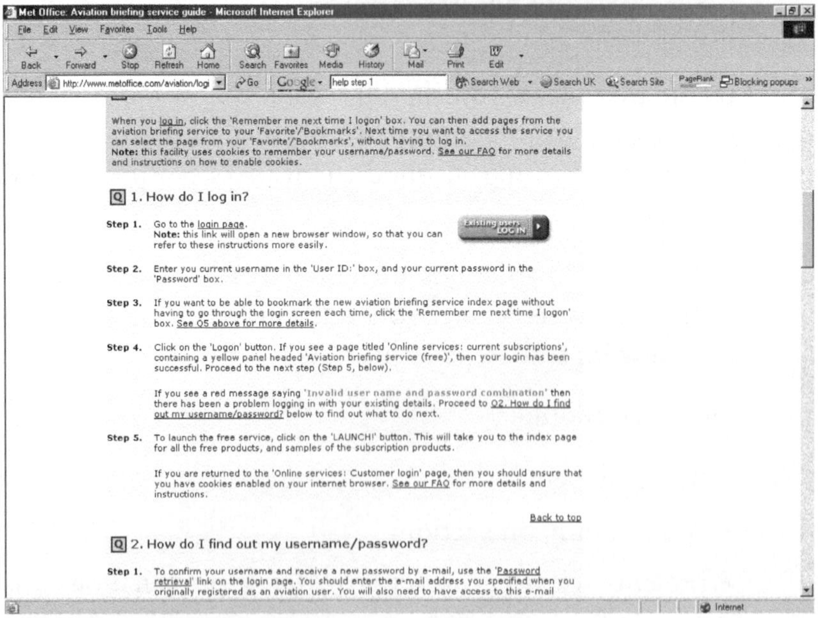

[Fig 5.12]

The clear, numbered steps within the Met Office's Aviation Service help section.

Keep content fresh

Once you've created the ideal content for your website and seen it published, that should not be viewed as the ending – it should be the beginning!

In time, your material will require to be **removed, archived** or **refreshed.**

If you revisit the articles on your website in this way (and are allowed to do so), your readers will appreciate its freshness while still being able to access useful, older material as required.

Summary

Despite the range of subjects you may have to cover when writing for websites, if you firmly establish **who** you are writing for and **why** and **follow the rules** above, you will naturally tailor your content to the needs of the ideal reader and achieve your specific goals.

Checklist – website writing

[ ] What are the goals?

[ ] What is the target audience?

[ ] What do my readers want?

[ ] What makes my topic (products, services, information) different?

[ ] What are the main benefits it can deliver?

[ ] Are there any secondary benefits?

[ ] Have I emphasized the benefits?

[ ] Have I made the value to the reader clear?

[ ] Have I answered the question 'What's in it for me'?

[ ] Have I answered the readers' needs?

[ ] What are my readers' questions or problems or objections?

[ ] Have I answered them?

[ ] Have I given answers before explanations?

[ ] Have I given summaries before details?

[ ] Have I given conclusions before discussions?

[ ] Did I examine competitors' sites?

[ ] Have I used the active voice?

[ ] Is my content useful, informative and credible?

[ ] Is key information easy to access?

[ ] Is key information, short, sharp and easy to consume?

[ ] Is my material up-to-date?

[ ] Have I included details of any features/specifications?

[ ] In instructions, have I told the reader what to do?

[ ] Are any actions simple to follow?

[ ] Does any About Us page tell the readers what you can do for them?

[ ] Have I created a Privacy Policy which is easy to read and understand while also reflecting the tone of your other content?

[ ] Have I created a useful set of FAQs?

[ ] Does each page show the reader where they are located?

When something can be read without effort, great effort has gone into its writing.

— Enrique Jardiel Poncela

CHAPTER 6 Writing for Email

Overview

If content is king, nowhere is this more obvious than within the email marketing arena. Permission-based email marketing is the killer application, IF used **correctly** and **creatively**.

Chapter objectives

Through this chapter, you will gain an end-to-end understanding of the ideal approach to copywriting and editing for email. As well as body content, this includes other essential elements such as header fields and formatting.

Chapter structure

- Introduction
- Content planning
- Content management
- Reader preferences
- Reader retention
- The 'From' header
- Subject lines
- Body content
- Action verbs and hyperlinks
- Personality
- Tone
- P.S. and signature files
- Spam words
- Email formats
- Frequency and timing
- Legislation
- Summary
- Checklist.

Introduction

Benefits offered by newsletters (e-zines) and email include:

- they are quicker and cheaper to create than offline direct communication;
- speed of (two-way) response;
- targeting according to user preferences;
- personalization;
- immediately trackable and measurable;
- the 'buzz' factor – users can share the message with others at the click of a button;
- Niche areas of interest can be reached.

The main difference between a newsletter and a single, commercial email is:

- A single, commercial email is usually intended to elicit an immediate action, usually a sale or a registration.
- A newsletter is a regular, scheduled communication which is useful to the recipient on an ongoing basis.

Both can transform a website into a portable tradeshow stand that travels to customer locations, instead of making the customer go to the show (**push** instead of **pull**).

Like stands, marketing emails and newsletters grab the attention of customers and draw them in to learn more about information, products and services.

Organizations implement email strategies for a number of reasons. And, before you begin writing, you need to be clear about the strategic objective.

This can include:

Adding Value to Products or Services: An email can serve as a support mechanism for a product or service.

Building Relationships: Building a relationship takes time and newsletter publishing is one avenue towards doing so.

Building Reputations: Newsletter publishing can create or strengthen the publisher's credibility and its position as being the 'expert'.

Community Building: Loyal recipients gain the feeling of being part of the publisher's community. This is particularly strengthened by reflecting their interests and responding to feedback.

Establishing Trust: Publishing a newsletter helps to establish the publisher as being reputable and, over time, inspires trust.

Gaining Feedback: Recipients can become a ready-made focus group. Reader surveys, polls and questionnaires can be used to discover more about the target market and help to shape existing or future products or services.

Generating Revenue: Generating revenue is one of the most common email marketing and newsletter publishing goals, through both customer retention and acquisition. Sources of email revenue include advertising/sponsorship, the direct sales of products or services, affiliate revenue and subscription fees (Fig. 6.1).

Information Sharing: Email is a most effective means of sharing information and knowledge. While email is often seen as a one-to-one form of communication, in this case the nature is one-to-many (and then many more as recipients pass along the content to friends and associates).

List Building: A growing list of opt-in email subscribers constantly increases the attentive audience, who can be targeted for any of the reasons listed here.

Networking and Making Contacts: Publishing a newsletter is an effective way to virtually meet people and build contact lists.

[Fig.6.1]
The Left Foot Company used email to boost business.
http://www.leftfootcompany.com.
Creatives and deployment by MediaCo (http://www.media.co.uk).

Promoting Products and Services: Email is often used as a vehicle for increasing the brand awareness of an organization, its products or services.

Promoting Thoughts or Opinions: Newsletters are often used as a vehicle to promote and spread ideas, thoughts and comment.

Supporting a Website: A newsletter can act as a strong, regular reminder to recipients – encouraging them to frequently use and revisit a website.

Whatever the objective, you face the challenge of creating something that people **anticipate, open, read** and **pass along** enthusiastically and that, at the end of the day, makes a measurable differences to themselves or their organization.

NOTE

According to an E-Dialog E-Mail Marketing Benchmarking Study, when asked: *'What is the primary goal of your email marketing efforts'*, the response was:

Acquire new customers:	**39%**
Deepen relationships with existing customers:	**33%**
Sell products/services:	**18%**
Disseminate information:	**7%**
Shorten purchase cycle:	**3%**

Content planning

From an editorial perspective, a good approach to content planning is to create an editorial calendar for the year ahead. This **Advance Feature Planning** involves the identification of likely topics/themes and possible sources of content for each mailout.

For example, seasons and events are often used as its basis. But flexibility should still be built-in to allow for the inclusion of topical or new information.

Content management

With regard to Content Management, workflow practices should be established. A typical approach would be:

- Create advance feature plan (see above).
- Discuss/agree current email content.
- Create content.

- Review/edit first draft of content.
- Review/edit second draft of content.
- Produce finished content.
- Integrate with design (plain text formatting or placement within HTML).

Also, some level of automation may be possible with regard to integration with an in-house Content Management System (CMS).

For example, as you create content for publication on a website, it could be flagged and routed elsewhere for inclusion in an email or, if technically possible within the system, inserted within an HTML template.

Reader preferences

While, in the first place, most organizations begin an email and newsletter publishing strategy with a 'one size to fit all' approach, stronger response rates can be gained through the future delivery of content relevant to readers' preferences.

Remember, the email will be competing with **ALL** other emails (personal, business, marketing AND spam) for space and attention in the In Box of the reader.

Therefore, if you can **build a profile** of your typical readers' preferences and the deployment system allows for segmentation, you can modify your content accordingly.

For example:

- You might create a different introduction paragraph for each identified sector.
- The subject line may be tailored to your reader.
- Your readers may be led to different landing pages.
- Your readers may be delivered content in their native language (Figs 6.2 and 6.3).

[Fig. 6.2]
La Gardenia Europa conducted a multi-lingual campaign including English and Spanish.
http://www.theartolivinginspain.com

Reader retention

People are persuaded to stay subscribed and continue reading newsletters through:

- **Professionalism** (email production and management)
- **Value** (the usefulness and relevance of content)

[Fig. 6.3]
La Gardenia Europa's Spanish version.
Creatives and deployment by MediaCo (http://www.media.co.uk).

- **Personality** (of the content and presentation)
- **Trust** (in the reputation of the sender).

A professional, valuable, personable publication will build the kind of:

- **Trust**,
- **Credibility** and
- **Loyalty** . . .

[Fig. 6.4]
Scottish Extra – a regular newsletter distributed by the Scottish Executive.
http://www.scotland.gov.uk/
Creatives and deployment by MediaCo (http://www.media.co.uk).

Required to:

- **Gain**,
- **Retain**,
- **Influence** and
- **Impact** . . .

. . . readers and customers.

[Fig. 6.5]

Experian used email and a viral game to raise awareness of its presence at the Technology for Marketing show.

http://www.experian.com/

Creatives and deployment by MediaCo (http://www.media.co.uk).

Of course, as with the other forms of online content we are exploring, the email should once again answer the **Who, What, When, How** questions to:

- say the right thing,
- in the right way,

- at the right time,
- to the right person . . .

. . . in order to get the **right results**.

NOTE

Forrester Research claims that approximately 50 per cent of email recipients read only the **first few sentences** of their email messages before deciding whether to read on.

And according to Jupiter Communications' research, only 15 per cent of web users read all email messages in their entirety.

Content

No matter what technologies are used for content management, list management, distribution and reporting, it is **your content** which will dictate whether the email is **opened**, well-received and **sought-after**.

It, too, has to pass the AIDAS test:

- Grab their **Attention**.
  For example, through your Subject Line.
- Activate their **Interest**.
  Getting your message across in the right tone.
- Elicit their **Desire**.
  Building your case and making the benefits crystal clear.
- Call them to **Action**.
  They read, respond and interact – the key goal.
- Deliver their **Satisfaction**.

They have gained a useful result and will look forward to future communications.

KEY ELEMENTS

The 'From' Header

This gives the recipient an immediate identifier as to the source of the communication. Addresses like mailer@alistservice.com should be avoided as they present the risk of being deleted or filtered out as spam.

It is much better to **identify yourself** as an individual. For example:

From: David Mill, MediaCo <david.mill@media.co.uk>

If it's not possible to use an individual's name, a **recognizable organization** will be acceptable. For example:

From: Google Alert <alert@googlealert.com>

And, if your organization's name isn't particularly recognizable but it or its URL are **descriptive** with regard to what you offer, that can work for you, too. For example:

From: Search Engine Specialists <info@search-engine-specialists.com>

Subject lines

Your Subject Line can serve numerous purposes. They include:

- identifying the source of the email;
- identifying the email contents;
- providing a reference for filtering/searching;
- providing a reference for browsing past issues;
- encouraging recipients to open and read the contents.

The last element – **encouraging recipients to open and read the contents** – is the most important and requires careful consideration.

This is also bearing in mind that some readers may not see more than the **first 35 characters** of the subject line, depending on their email set-up. Also, the Subject Line should never be longer than 60 characters.

Personalization – for example using the recipient's name (Dear David) at the start of the text – if used judicially, can also increase open rates.

NOTE

In an e-Dialog email Marketing Benchmarking Study, 45 per cent of respondents said they gained better results through the usage of personalization.

However, as more spammers use personalization (David, here is your FREE Porsche) this may be better avoided in Subject Lines (which also allows more characters to be used for your actual subject).

Other **Subject Line techniques**:

- You can give news (Product X has been released).
- You can make an announcement (All Help files are now available to download).
- You can make the reader curious (Discover the secret to great Subject Lines . . .).
- You can ask a question (Do you know how to write great Subject Lines?).
- You can emphasize benefits (Here's how Product X will increase your sales).
- You can inject urgency (One day left to register for the Marketing Secrets event).

Body Content

You have some **10 seconds** to grab the attention of your recipient after they have opened the message. Therefore, your content should:

- **Be relevant and focused.**
  The more it appeals to your audience, the better the results.

- **Make the objective obvious.**
  For example, 'Enter our competition to win' or 'Here is the latest news on . . .'

- **Quickly highlight the benefits.**
  Offered by your information, products or services.

In addition, it's often good practice to take an early opportunity to tell the recipient why they are receiving the email. For example, 'You have received this newsletter because . . . '

With regard to the message itself, it should:

- **Be clear and concise.**
  Written in plain language.

- **Avoid jargon.**
  No buzzwords, jargon, funky phrases or punctuation unless expected by the target market.

- **Speak their language.**
  Adopting the right tone and personality for your intended audience.

- **Be kept short.**
  Short copy (maximum 500–700 words) gets results but, if it must be long, a synopsis or content list should be provided at the outset. HTML versions that can be viewed in one screen (600 pixels by 600 pixels) are also most effective. If they are longer, key elements should

be viewable 'above the fold'. As a guide to length, you should say as little as it takes to meet your objectives.

- **Be immediately of interest.**
  Having the key points and main click-through links in the immediately viewable area. **The Lead** – the first sentences you write – should summarize what you're writing about and why it should be of interest to the recipient.

- **Provoke action.**
  Higher links always gain higher click-throughs so a response mechanism should be included within the lead (initial paragraphs) or as soon as is practical in the email. You can seek other actions in the middle and end of the email.

- **Deliver the promise.**
  Whatever hook you've used to attract attention.
  Whatever reader expectations have been built.
  Whatever you've said in the Lead.
  This has to be clearly supported by whatever you write in the Body.

- **Be accurate.**
  If you fail to appear credible, your reader will quickly unsubscribe.

- **Be written in the style of a letter, not an ad.**
  This is a one-to-one communication – brash display advertising and sales pitches belong elsewhere.

- **Be genuine.**
  As with your website copy, there is no place for hype and marketese.

- **Be easily consumed by the skimming reader.**
  Use sub-headings and make them stand out and use bullets to make your most important points obvious and easy to read.

- **Be as consistent as possible with your website.** While your email may be more intimate and conversational than the content of your website, the gap between them should not be so large as to break a relationship you've worked hard to build.

NOTE

Many email software packages will initially display the **first 15–20 lines of copy**. What lies 'above the fold' without scrolling is, therefore, another key factor in capturing the interest of a recipient.

Generally speaking, your content should:

- be creative, so it stands out from the crowd;
- Be compelling – active voice and action verbs;
- talk about THEM not you;
- place them in the action;
- stress benefits not features;
- build real and perceived value;
- have personality – so you and the recipient 'connect'.

Action verbs and hyperlinks

The most important call to action in an email is usually **Click Here** (even if you don't actually use these words). And, when reviewing an email, you should ask yourself the questions:

- Is it obvious **where** they should click?
- Is it obvious **why** they should click?

The primary link should be near the start of the copy, with a further call to action in the middle and a reminder at the end.

In addition, the hyperlinks should use action verbs. For example:

- Get the guide to Online Copywriting.
- Discover the secrets of email marketing.
- Subscribe to the information-packed newsletter.

Personality

An email is most effective when it does one of two things:

1. Reflects your typical reader's personality.
2. Appeals to your reader at another level – that is, be a personality the reader can both recognize and accept within the context of the email.

This personality also adds to the human element of the email and boosts the one-to-one characteristic of email marketing – bearing in mind it's not an audience you're writing for, it's an individual sitting alone in front of a screen.

NOTE

According to a Forrester Consumer Technographics Benchmark Study, those interviewed unsubscribed from email lists for the following reasons:

Irrelevant:	55%
Too frequent:	52%
Poor content:	32%
Too long:	26%

Tone

As with writing for websites, your personality should be modified to the extent that you use a style of language your **typical reader** will understand and relate to. It is based on what they are like.

And your tone should be modified so it fits the role you wish to play. This is particularly true when writing for email.

Most of us write emails day in and day out to friends and colleagues. Within these communications, we're speaking as ourselves to people who know us.

They may be laced with humour, wry comments and tongue-in-cheek remarks. And, most often, we fully expect the recipients to read every word.

Your good friend or work mate wouldn't walk away when you were half way through a conversation? At least I hope not! But your online reader just might if you convey the wrong personality or tone.

Therefore, in commercial/marketing emails, your writing should:

- Be **calm**, **polite** and **professionally conversational**.
- Be **personable**.
  Beginning with something like 'Hello, Harry', 'Dear Sally', 'Hello from me [your name or company]'.

  Ending with something like 'Thanks for your time', 'Best wishes', 'Good luck', 'Regards'.

  Using 'you', 'I' and 'we'.
- Be in the **active voice**.
  That is, a sentence style in which the subject performs the action.

  'You will receive the fact sheet as soon as you complete the registration form' is much better than the corporately passive 'Access to the fact sheet will be gained after the registration form has been completed.'

It is also important to **modify your tone** according to the **nature of your message** even if it is to an audience you regularly email. For example, different tones would be used for:

- an alert,
- a Christmas greeting,
- a software enhancement.

And don't forget about the **KISS!** (Keep It Simple, Stupid!). In other words, speak one-to-one in your **reader's language**, **be brief** and **be specific**.

PS. and signature files

Once you've completed the content of your email, don't stop! A **PS.** and your signature file are powerful, too.

A short PS. will catch attention and increase click-throughs.

It can:

- summarize a benefit through an appropriate marketing slogan or description (free information, key products or useful services on your website);
- include a call to action if appropriate (a reason why the reader should contact you or visit your site).

This could, alternatively, be included in your **signature file** (otherwise known as your 'sig'), the tagline that is manually or automatically added to the bottom of your email.

Your signature file should:

- be short and simple and not be more than six to eight lines in length, with each line not being longer than 65 characters.
- be like a business card or letterhead, containing.

  your name

  your organization

contact information (phone and fax numbers)

your URL and email address

- summarize a benefit and/or include a call to action if not used within a P.S.

> NOTE
> If you are writing for different audiences or about different products or services, it will be useful to have a set of different, targeted signature files.

Exceptions to the rules

More often than not, you will produce more effective email by following the guidance here. However, they do say that rules are meant to be broken.

And sometimes, if you strike a perfect tone, you can actually wax lyrical in the knowledge your (even lengthy) narrative will be happily consumed.

For example, one of my own favourite newsletters comes sporadically from the producers of Laphroaig malt whisky. The first one I received stopped me in my tracks.

Not because of headings, bullet points or compelling calls to action. But because I thought it was an email from a personal acquaintance whose name I didn't initially recognize. In a way it was, as the key theme of the marketing activity is Friends of Laphroaig.

Here's one I received previously:

Subject: Laphroaig: A Father's Day Greeting

Dear David

I hope this letter finds you well. I wanted to take a moment of your time about a tradition that is strong here on Islay, and maybe for you as well – Father's Day.

Father's Day is traditionally the third Sunday in June and has become a day not only to honour your father but any man who has acted as a father figure to you. The very first Father's Day is thought to date back to 1910.

My Father was not home very much in my formative years, being in the Navy. He was the stranger that came home in the fancy uniform maybe twice a year. By the end of his leave my sisters and I were just getting to know this strong person when all of a sudden he was whisked away again.

But he was OUR DAD and in OUR OWN WAY we were proud of him, but we didn't really know him.

Eventually of course he did come home for good, but by this time I was very independent and at sea myself, before I realised my dad was getting older and was not always going to be around.

What made me realise how much I missed his presence was when I was told a story one Father's Day by a friend when we were sheltering from a storm in the Lake District. I was on leave, like my father. I hadn't even bothered to go home, preferring to go off and prove that I was still capable of being independent.

The friend's story went like this. One evening he waited up until his father returned from work, as he worked late nearly every night, and he asked him how much he was paid per hour at work. His father was taken aback at this and resented his son asking what he thought was a pretty personal question. He brushed him off and sent him to his room.

Later on he reflected and went to see his son and asked if he needed money for something. My friend said yes he needed money but could not give him an explanation of what it was for.

This annoyed his father and they parted in not too favourable terms until the next evening. My friend's father had been bothered all day thinking his son had got himself into some sort of financial predicament and was determined to find out what it was.

After some discussion he told his son he earned £10.00 per hour at work and did he need money for something. My friend said yes knowing that he now needed a loan of £5.00 pounds. His father was mystified but he gave him a 5-pound note. His son pulled another grubby 5 pound note from his pocket, and put it all together and asked his father if he could buy one hour of his time that evening!

This incident made me think of my relationship with my own father so on my way home I bought him a bottle of his favourite malt and I did that every Father's Day until the day he died.

Whilst I could never get back the years we missed I made up for it (as best you can) in his later life over a wee dram or two.

With this in mind, we are running a special offer in Oddbins with £2.50 off every bottle of my special 15-year-old Laphroaig. In addition, we are giving all of our online Friends of Laphroaig in the UK an extra £2.50 off a bottle via this coupon (see below).

You may use the coupon yourself or if you would like to send it to someone for this special day just send it with one of the Father's Day E-cards we have made for you. Hoping you have a special Father's Day.

Slainte
Iain

To print or send your voucher click here.

Send a Laphroaig E-card to your father click here.

[Fig. 6.6]
The Friends of Laphroaig (FOL) theme.

It works for me. And it works for them because it's consistent with the theme of their online strategy and is tailored to an understanding they clearly have of their targeted consumers (Fig. 6.6).

Not many would get away with it but it illustrates that opportunities exist – or can be created – to occasionally and successfully buck the trend.

The Laphroaig website:
http://www.laphroaig.com/

PS: I only have the occasional tipple – honest. Slainte! (Gaelic meaning: 'health!').

Spam words

While used less by business recipients, online email service providers like Hotmail and Yahoo! are using Junk and Adult Content Filters in an attempt to protect their users from spam.

Here is the **Microsoft description** of some of the 'junk' words filters looked for and where the filter looks for them.

- First eight characters of From are digits.
- Subject contains 'advertisement'.

- Body contains 'money back'.
- Body contains 'cards accepted'.
- Body contains 'removal instructions'.
- Body contains 'extra income'.
- Subject contains '!' AND Subject contains '£'.
- Subject contains '!' AND Subject contains 'free'.
- Body contains ',000' AND Body contains '!!'.
- AND Body contains '£'.
- Body contains 'Dear friend'.
- Body contains 'for free?'.
- Body contains 'for free!'.
- Body contains 'Guarantee' AND (Body contains 'satisfaction' OR Body contains 'absolute').
- Body contains 'more info' AND Body contains 'visit'.
- AND Body contains '£'.
- Body contains 'SPECIAL PROMOTION'.
- Body contains 'one-time mail'.
- Subject contains '££'.
- Body contains '£££'.
- Body contains 'order today'.
- Body contains 'order now!'.
- Body contains 'money-back guarantee'.
- Body contains '100% satisfied'.
- To contains 'friend@'.
- To contains 'public@'.
- To contains 'success@'.
- From contains 'sales@'.
- From contains 'success.'.

- From contains 'success@'.
- From contains 'mail@'.
- From contains '@public'.
- From contains '@savvy'.
- From contains 'profits@'.
- From contains 'hello@'.
- Body contains 'mlm'.
- Body contains '@mlm'.
- Body contains '///////////////'.
- Body contains 'cheque or money order'.

Email formats

Possible email formats include:

- **Plain text.**
  Straight text with line breaks.
- **Enhanced text.**
  Text in which you can add text styling (**bold**, *italic*, etc).
- **HTML.**
  Fully designed graphical look and feel.
- **Rich media.**
  Animation, audio, DHTML etc.

And some considerations you should give to them are:

Plain text (Fig. 6.7)

- Simple to implement.
- All recipients can view it whatever their email software.
- Small file size so download is fast.

Walking and Hiking special
Highlights this month:

Competition >>

Seven nights in a North North Devonshire cottage are up for grabs.
http://www.stanfords-newsletter.co.uk#competition

Springtime Offers >>

Our Times and Michelin Atlases offers.
http://www.stanfords-newsletter.co.uk#special

The Pembrokeshire Coast >>

Jim's walking and hiking guide to the Pembrokeshire Coast and plan your own walking holiday.
http://www.stanfords-newsletter.co.uk#pembrokeshire

Climbing Aconcagua >>

Read Alex Stewart's account of his brother's ascent of the highest mountain in the west.
http://www.stanfords-newsletter.co.uk#aconcagua

[Fig. 6.7]
Plain text email – from Stanfords Maps and Books.
http://www.stanfords.co.uk

Enhanced text (Fig. 6.8)

- Your headings and calls to action can be emphasized.
- Links can be in plain English.
  For example, 'Visit our company' rather than:
  Click below to visit our company
  http://mail.mail01.co.uk/cgi-bin/nph-t.pl?U = 252&M=135306&MS= 3461
- Smaller file size than full HTML.

HTML (Fig. 6.9)

- You can create a more distinctive look and feel.
- Greater functionality.

W@W ... just a few days left...

UK E-commerce Awards: closing deadline 5pm Friday
www.scottish-enterprise.com/ecommerceawards2004

If your website strategy is making your business more competitive, then:

- You could win up to £40,000
- You could increase your company profile nationally
- You could seriously increase business
- You could get a free place at the gala dinner in Glasgow

The closing date for entries to the UK E-Commerce Awards (previously Winners @ Web) is **this Friday 30 July**, at **5pm** and it's **easy to apply** online. So why not apply today?

It's a great chance for Scottish companies like yours to **raise the profile of your business** across the UK.

Find out more about previous winners.

There's a category for everyone - from sole traders to larger organisations:

- Best e-business start-up
- Best e-business
- Best e-trading
- Best use of broadband
- Best use of teleworking

Competition finalists report that they've won **more business**, just by association with the awards. Couple that with free attendance for finalists at the gala awards dinner in September, and you can't lose.

Apply online today.

[Fig. 6.8]
Enhanced text email – reproduced with the permission of Scottish Enterprises
http://www.scottish-enterprise.com/

- More polished.
- Stronger branding.

But . . .

– Not all email software can read HTML.

– Some users don't want to receive HTML (and switch off the capability in their software).

– Larger file size so longer download (recommended size is max. 25 K).

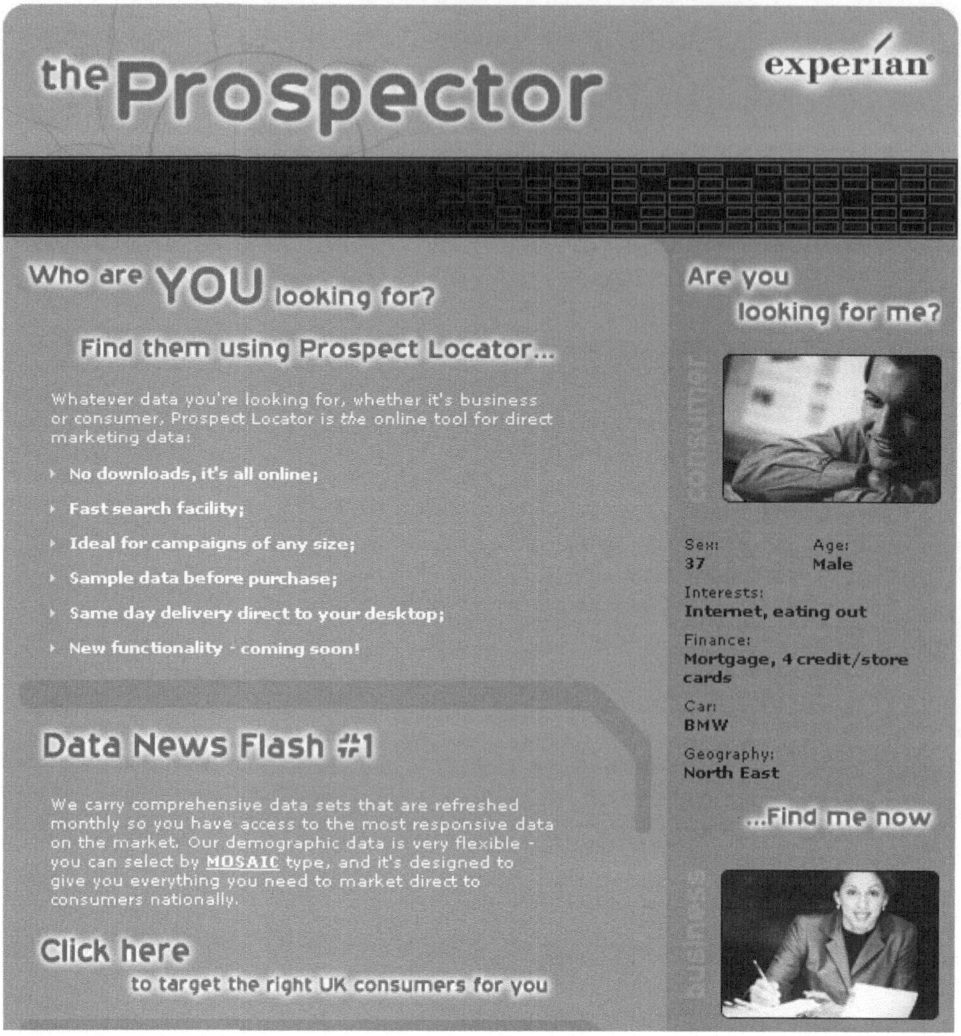

[Fig. 6.9]
HTML email – from experían.
http://www.experian.com

- Most often has to be read while connected to the Internet.
- Forwarding not always simple (with messages becoming garbled in transmission).
- Can be blocked by corporate firewalls (Internet security systems).

Rich media

Often provides a dynamic user experience, but:

- Not viewable by all recipients.
- Not wanted by many recipients (e.g. someone in an office most likely doesn't want to have Colonel Bogey blasting out when they check their mail).
- Often requires a higher bandwidth and, therefore, can be slow to download.
- Can be blocked by corporate firewalls (Internet security systems).

Plain Text with Landing Page(s)

If your recipients' preferences are not known (that is, they haven't explicitly stated a desire to receive email in HTML or rich media formats) or as a standard policy to avoid the current drawbacks of richer emails, a recommended approach is to write for Plain Text format with a supporting web-based landing page or area (Fig. 6.10).

The benefits offered by using **landing pages** include:

- More depth for your content – the landing area can be split into sections.
- More space – rather than being confined by the email software's viewable screen.
- The messages can be significantly expanded upon.
- More sophisticated.
- Can use features not supported by email applications.
- More ways of linking to the additional content within the parent site.
- In addition, a web-based Newsletter area can become a strong resource within the parent site itself.

[Fig. 6.10]

A landing page that supported Stanfords' plain text email.

http://www.stanfords.co.uk

Creatives and deployment by MediaCo (http://www.media.co.uk).

Frequency and timing

When writing and planning the content of your email, you should give thought to frequency and timing.

It's generally believed that a frequency greater than **twice a month** – unless your recipient has signed up for more frequent updates – is excessive and will increase the number of unsubscribers.

However, it is possible to provide customers with the **option** of receiving regular updates (for example, businesses information alerts).

NOTE A DoubleClick Consumer email Study found the majority of people (some 60 per cent) preferred to receive business news on a weekly basis.

A point to note regarding frequency is the **more frequent** the email is, **the shorter** it should be. People will happily open a short list of daily business updates but few will want to receive pages of information at this frequency.

There are, in fact, numerous theories about the best day of the week to deliver your message. Some recommend targeting consumers over the weekend, some recommend avoiding Fridays for business-to-business communications.

Certainly, different **days of the week** and **hours of the day** are important for different audiences.

For example, an entertainment site is likely to do better sending an email on Friday afternoon or during the weekend. A business news alert would do better early in the morning (but not in the morning of Monday or anytime on Friday).

However, in general, emails that focus on a business market should be sent during the **middle of the business week**, between late in the day Monday and Thursday afternoon.

The goal is to avoid the Monday morning 'inbox glut', as well as Friday afternoon when some business people have already mentally 'checked out' for the weekend.

This includes business emails that feature news, products or services of interest to other business personnel. You need their **full attention** and their **time**, and you are most likely to get it during the heart of the business week.

Best approach is to test to see what day (or days) of the week yield higher response rates.

NOTE

DoubleClick's Internal Benchmark Statistics reveal that Tuesday is the best day for Marketing messages and Tuesday or Wednesday are best for Information Publishing. 10 a.m. is seen as the best time of day to broadcast.

Another option is to ask subscribers **at the time of registration** when and how often they'd like to receive email. In addition, one choice you can offer is the provision of a less frequent digest version.

What is **most important** is that the content you create is of **definite interest** to your reader. It's their level of interest which will have the greatest impact on the how frequently they will be happy to hear from you.

Legislation

Egg and spam – bacon and spam – egg, bacon, sausage and spam – spam, bacon, sausage and spam, spam, spam, spam . . .

– creative writing from the Monty Python team!

But we all know too much Spam is a huge problem and we have a challenge as writers to find a welcome place within our readers' mail boxes.

Therefore, while, in the first place, your focus will be on the **creative aspects** of your email activity, it will also be useful for you to understand the **legal aspects** of commercial email communications.

In a bid to reduce the problem of Spam – or Unsolicited Commercial email (UCE) – new regulations came into force in the UK in December 2003. Anyone who sends direct marketing messages by email must comply with these rules or face possible prosecution for each breach.

- Who can you email?
- In what circumstances?
- What is best practice?

Here is a guide to help you understand the rights and wrongs and best practice surrounding email marketing.

What the law requires

1. You cannot transmit unsolicited marketing material by email to **an individual subscriber** (a consumer) unless the recipient has previously notified you, the sender, that he or she **consents**, for the time being, to receive such communications.

   Exceptions to this rule:

   a. The recipient has **actively invited** the communication via a third party.

   b. The recipient has been **made aware** he or she is likely to receive marketing messages but **has not**, for the time being, objected to receiving them (through a simple and clear method).

2. You cannot transmit any marketing email (whether solicited or unsolicited) to any subscriber (whether corporate or individual) where

   a. the identity of the sender has been **disguised or concealed**, or

   b. a **valid address** to which the recipient can send an opt-out request has not been provided.

Definition of an individual subscriber

A **subscriber** is defined in the regulations as 'a person who is party to a contract with a provider of public electronic communications for the supply of such services'. They will have an email address like:

theirname@afreeservice.com

An **individual** is defined as 'a living individual' (that is, not a corporation). A living person who works for a corporation will not be a party to a telecoms/ISP contract; the corporation will be.

Therefore, **corporations** and **employees of corporations** may be sent marketing emails even if they have not consented to them.

Please note, however, that marketing emails should be restricted to 'business products or services'.

Is explicit consent always required?

Other than when the exceptions apply in 'What the law requires' (above) you may send email for marketing purposes to an individual subscriber **without explicit consent** where:

1. you have obtained the contact details of the recipient in the **course of a sale** or **negotiations for the sale** of a product or service to the recipient;
2. the marketing material you are sending is in respect of your similar products and services only; and
3. the recipient has been given a simple and clear means of **refusing** (free of charge except for the cost of transmission) the use of their contact details at the time those details were **initially collected** and at the time of each subsequent communication.

This is known as '**soft opt-in**'.

The course of a sale or negotiations for the sale

Where a person has actively expressed an interest in purchasing a product or service and **not opted out** of receiving future related marketing messages (having been given a **clear opportunity** to do so), the company can continue to send them marketing material by email until that person opts out.

Opt-out requests

No matter the means that consent may have been obtained and despite interpretation of the course of a sale or negotiations for the sale, particular attention is being paid to **failures to comply** with opt-out requests.

In other words, while the recipient may, directly or indirectly, have given consent, that has to be considered to be **for the time being**.

And it is essential that they be given the **clear opportunity to easily remove that consent** (to opt out) in every subsequent communication.

From the Information Commissioner's guidance: 'We will take **enforcement action** against those companies within the UK jurisdiction who persistently **fail to comply with opt-out requests** from individual subscribers'.

When an opt-out request is received, the contact details should be 'suppressed' rather than deleted. This will ensure that person's request is recorded, retained and respected until such time as that person may provide new consent. This would also be useful evidence in the event of a complaint.

Lists compiled prior to December 2003

If these lists were compiled in accordance with privacy legislation in force at the time (e.g. the Data Protection

Act 1998) **AND have been used recently**, they can continue to be used unless the recipient has opted out.

Business to business communication

Only individuals (see 'Definition of an individual subscriber' above) have the enforceable right of opt-out under the new regulations.

However, where the sending of marketing material to the employee of a company includes the **processing of personal data** (i.e. the marketer knows the name of the recipient), that individual has a right, under the Data Protection Act 1998, to request that no further material is sent.

And a valid address must be provided to which the recipient can send an opt-out request.

So, an **individual** would be, for example:

person@theirhome.com

And an **identifiable employee** would be:

person_name@theircompany.com

Best practice

1. If email addresses are to be used for marketing purposes, this should be **clearly stated** at the point of collection.
2. Once informed, the user should be able to **refuse permission** for their email to be used for marketing purposes (i.e. opt out).
3. If email is to be sent to those with whom a customer relationship exists, the content should be in reference to **similar products and services**.

4. If the email addresses are to be shared with third parties, this should be clearly stated at the **point of collection**.
5. Email addresses **should not be harvested** (e.g. copied from websites) and used for marketing purposes without the recipients' knowledge.
6. Recipients should be able to **refuse permission** for further marketing messages to be sent to them at any time.
7. Your identity as the sender should never be **disguised** or **concealed**.
8. In **every** communication, recipients must be given a simple and clear means of **opting out** from receiving future emails.
9. When an opt-out request is received it **must be honoured**, with the contact details ideally being 'suppressed' rather than deleted.

The above is modified from a Fact Sheet I wrote for Scottish Enterprise. That and other e-business information can be accessed at:

http://www.scottish-enterprise.com/factsheets/

Resources

The Privacy and Electronic Communications (EC Directive) Regulations 2003 See Regulations 22 and 23
http://www.hmso.gov.uk/si/si2003/20032426.htm

The Committee of Advertising Practice
http://www.cap.org.uk

Privacy Guidelines from the Information Commissioner's Office.
http://www.informationcommissioner.gov.uk

Final words On email

'**Test**', '**test**' and '**test**' again! And 'learn'.

From fields, subject lines, introductions, formats, PS. contents to signature files, **all elements** of your email should be thoroughly tested and reviewed according to results analysis and feedback.

Not only do you have to capture your recipients' attention, you have to retain it – testing and learning and then modifying your approach will help you to achieve both.

Summary

While spam has become an increasing problem, email is a hugely effective channel. If you give people **what they want**, **when they want it**, in **the format they prefer**, they will welcome your messages and allow you space within their precious mailboxes.

Checklist – writing for email

[ ] Am I clear about the objectives of my email?

[ ] Have I created something that people will anticipate [ ], open [ ], read [ ] and pass along [ ]?

[ ] Have I created an Advance Feature Plan?

[ ] Have I built a profile of my readership?

[ ] Can content be tailored to and segmented for different reader preferences and, if so, have I created different versions?

[ ] Does my email deliver professionalism [ ], value [ ], personality [ ], trust [ ]?

[ ] Will my content grab attention [ ], activate interest [ ], elicit desire [ ], call readers to action [ ], deliver satisfaction [ ]?

[ ] Have I used an effective From Header?

[ ] Have I used an effective Subject Line?

[ ] Is my Body content relevant and focused?

[ ] Have I made the objectives clear?

[ ] Are the benefits to the reader obvious?

[ ] Have I stressed benefits rather than features?

[ ] Have I written in plain language?

[ ] Have I avoided jargon?

[ ] Have I used active verbs within hyperlinks?

[ ] Is the tone and personality right for the audience?

[ ] Is the tone and personality right for the subject matter?

[ ] Have I talked about the reader rather than me or us?

[ ] Have I used the active voice?

[ ] Have I written to the correct length?

[ ] Is the content immediately of interest?

[ ] Have I summarized the content in the first few sentences?

[ ] Have I provoked action at the beginning, in the middle and at the end of the email?

[ ] Have I delivered the promise?

[ ] Is my content accurate?

[ ] Have I written in the style of a letter and not an ad?

[ ] Has hype and marketese been avoided?

[ ] Is the content easily consumed by the skimming reader?

[ ] Is my writing consistent with the language of the website?

[ ] Have I used an effective PS?

[ ] Have I used an effective signature file?

[ ] Have I avoided the use of spam words?

[ ] Is the correct format being used?

[ ] Have I established the ideal frequency and timing?

[ ] Does my strategy comply with current legislation?

[ ] Is there another way in which I can successfully be more different?

[ ] Have I tested, tested and tested and made any required changes?

The perfect love affair is one which is conducted entirely by post.

— George Bernard Shaw

CHAPTER 7

Writing for Search Engines

Overview

Meta Tags, SERPs, algorithms, spiders, robots . . . and you thought this book was about writing and editing online! Well, it is, and the successful online copywriter or editor should have, at least, a fundamental understanding of how **the use of words influences search engine positioning.**

This isn't a DIY guide to perfect search engine optimization* – that's best left to a specialist. However, it does provide a guide to how words really matter when it comes to gaining prominent positions in the SERPS (Search Engine Results Pages).

And why is this important? Because, with more than 250 million searches being conducted every day on Google alone, you will want readers to find your words – and website – before those of others!

Chapter objectives

After reading this chapter you will be able to write and organize copy which is both useful to readers and 'search engine friendly' – meaning the words are used and structured for best search engine placement. Meta Tags (elements of code read by some search engines) are also explained.

* Search engine optimization involves techniques that are used on websites in order to rank favourably within search engines for targeted words and phrases. This is primarily achieved through the manipulation of visible content, code and site structure.

Chapter structure

- Introduction
- Body Text
- Title and Meta Tags
- Alt Text
- Off-the-page factors
- Summary
- Checklist.

Introduction

There is much talk about search engine algorithms (the closely guarded 'recipes' that search engines use to decide how to rank the results of a given search).

However, the critical element is *not* $PR(A) = (1 - d) + d \times [PR(T1)/C(T1) + \cdots + PR(Tn)/C(Tn)]$ . . .

. . . it's the **written word** – yahoo, say all of us!

Yes, folks, it's *our writing* that again makes the difference. And, although a specialist search engine optimizer will add to and modify our works, we can minimize these adjustments (and we'd really prefer they didn't happen at all!) while, at the same time, actually making our copy **better for readers.**

This chapter will take you through the key rules that apply to the main search engines.

Body Text

Search engines just love the words we weave within the Body Text of web pages and **nothing** has a stronger influence on positioning.

An ideal target is some **300–500 words per page**, and keyword phrases (those word combinations most likely to be used by people searching for the kind of information you are publishing) used consistently throughout your body text will boost rankings.

And, once again, it's **the initial material** (the lead statement – the first two-to-three paragraphs and especially the first 150–250 characters) which is most important.

Of course, if those relevant phrases are important for search engines, they must be important for readers, too. So where else should they be than near the beginning? Doh! We're starting to see a theme here!

In addition, as with good content practice in general, when possible the targeted key phrases should appear at the start or **near the start of paragraphs**.

TIP

Target phrases, not single words

Please note, your emphasis should be placed on **phrases**, not single words.

For example, when I searched on Google (UK) for 'marketing', I was presented with millions of results covering a wide range of marketing-related information sources. But I was really looking for 'web marketing guide'. By refining my search, I was then able to select from a smaller list of **more relevant** results.

That's what all searchers do and what we should bear in mind when writing.

At a Jupiter Ad Forum in New York, Ted Meisel, CEO of Overture, shared his view on search engine keyword length data. He indicated that, based on Overture internal data, the percentage of search words in a search query is getting longer:

- 1-word queries: 19%
- 2-word queries: 23%
- 3-word queries: 24%
- 4-word queries: 15%
- 5-word queries: 19%

The above data indicates 58 per cent of searchers are entering three keywords or more.

And, on many fronts, good practice for search engines is good practice for readers, too. For example, how often have you seen links like:

- Click here for information about MediaCo's services.

Hello, what kind of services? Better would be something like:

- Online marketing services provided by MediaCo – useful information.

And, yes, when it comes to links, many search engines consider the text **in and around hyperlinks** to be more important, which is why I've presented the keywords in the above sentence as the hyperlink.

Meaningful sub-headings and emphasis

Again, as we know, online readers tend to initially skim text rather than read every word so sub-headings and **emphasis** draw them to key areas or important content.

And, guess what, it works for search engines, too. They assume more importance is being placed on phrases in

bold and within headings (which a web developer will appropriately tag e.g. <H3>**Heading here**</H3>), and phrases used in this way will help boost positioning if they match users' searches.

Another way to make effective use of your targeted search phrases while also assisting (those skimming, scanning) readers is to include them within bullet lists. For example:

MediaCo's **online marketing services** include:

- <u>Search Engine Marketing</u>;
- <u>Email Marketing</u>;
- <u>Strategic Link Building</u>;
- <u>Website copywriting</u>; and
- <u>Viral [buzz] marketing</u>.

But, beware, do not try to stuff every possible search phrase into one piece of copy or a single page. The **shotgun approach just does not work.** From a search engine perspective, this would simply dilute the weight of the individual phrases and it's most likely to appear clumsy to your readers.

Rather, **organize your content logically** with, ideally, each page being focused on a single topic and material split into **separate pages** or **sections.** This will assist your readers and allow the correct emphasis to be placed on targeted phrases – **best practice is three to five targeted phrases per page.**

Also, don't be tempted to be over-repetitive simply in an attempt to shovel your key phrases into short or early copy.

For example, I doubt if you would be comfortable reading or writing this:

Content is King (Writing and Editing Online) is about effective writing and editing for online. This guide on editing and writing online is an essential resource for anyone wishing to improve their writing and editing online. Writing and editing online – the guide.

Google-eyed? Unfortunately, this misguided 'shuffle the words' approach is adopted by some who have no respect for written words or the people likely to read them.

A craftsperson will achieve better results by weaving the words much more effectively.

TIP

Keyphrase research

While, of course, you will be well aware of the subject matter on which you are writing, you may not always know what phrases people are using to find such material by way of the search engines.

It is, therefore, important to conduct some keyphrase research at the outset. Useful online tools include:

Wordtracker

http://www.wordtracker.com
This is a keyphrase evaluation tool that gives popularity figures for individual search terms based upon actual search engine activity.

Overture's term suggestion tool

http://www.uk.overture.com
This reveals search terms related to subject matter, including how many times they were searched during the previous month.

Title and Meta Tags

The Title Tag and Meta Tags are HTML tags giving information about a web page. They are inserted within the code and the content of the Title Tag is what you see at the top of your browser.

The two meta tags that some search engines read are the **meta keywords** tag and the **meta description** tag.

Visitors don't see these tags unless they view the source code of the page.

Title Tag

<TITLE> Content is King, Writing & Editing Online. Marketers, Copywriters & Editors</TITLE>

Try to use up to 10 words but, if necessary, use up to 15. NB: the first 60 characters (including punctuation and spaces) are the most crucial.

Not only does the Title Tag appear at the top of the web pages, it's the link (often along with the description-below) people see in search results. For example:

france maps, books, regional touring guides – france travel

Plan touring holidays with **France maps**, travel guides, cycling guides, hotel accommodation guides – tourism guides. . . . www.france-travel.co.uk

(Fig.7.1)

So, well-written Title Tags will result in more clicks.

> NOTE
> The Title Tag is a key influencer of search engine positioning. Therefore, it should be varied on each page to reflect the specific content it heads.

Description Tag

(Important to use as the content can be presented as the summary of your page within some search engine results. For example, often in Google – see Fig. 7.1.)

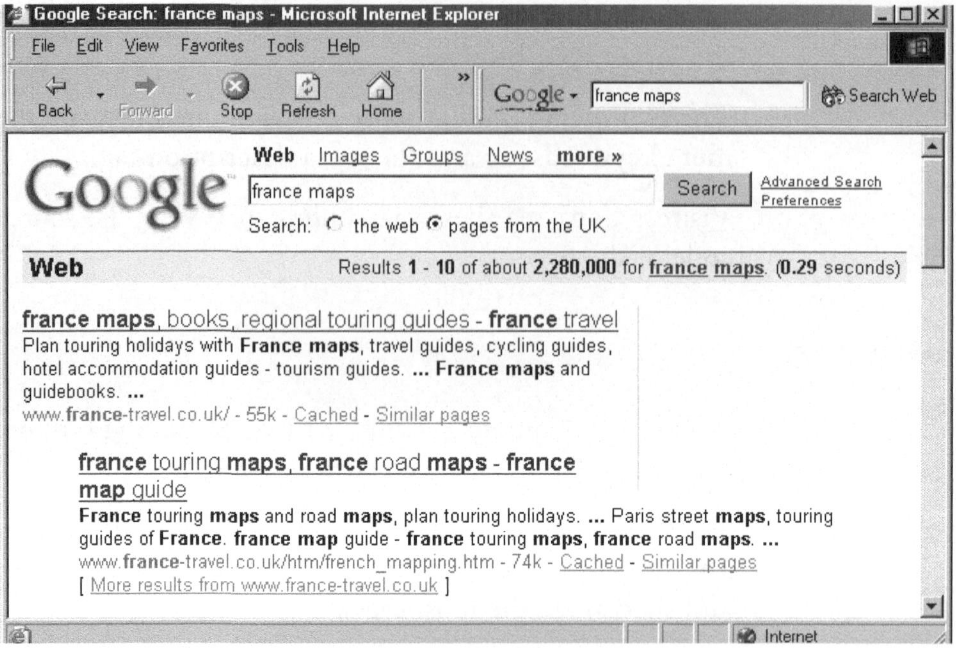

[Fig. 7.1]
How the Title Tag appears in Google's results as a clickable link.

<META name="description" content="Content is King-Writing & Editing Online. Guide for Marketers, copywriters, editors. Covers copywriting, sub-editing, websites, email, search engines, ezines, newsletters, ads, banners, ads, pay per click, sms . . .">

The Description Tag should include targeted search phrases – but keep the important keywords at the beginning and try not to use more than 200 characters (including punctuation and spaces).

Keywords Tag

(Less important at present, as often ignored by the major search engines).

<META name="keywords" content="Content is King, writing editing online, guide, book, writing, editing,

online, internet, marketer, copywriting, sub-editing, editor, book, websites, email, search engines, ezines, newsletters, online ads, banners, pay per click, ads, business to business, business to consumer, david mill, advertisement, banner, sms, blogs">

Use the most important keyphrases first and use each keyword no more than three times, include plurals. The Keywords Tag should contain fewer than 1000 characters (including punctuation and spacing) although **no gain** will be achieved if a keyword or phrase is not also used within the body text of the page.

NOTE

Deeper search engine optimization

If you do venture deeper into search engine territory, you will encounter commentary about keyword density, relevance, stemming and so on. And, by then, you will most probably either retreat to your writing zone or plunge on into the inner depths of search engine optimization.

Either way, you will realize what matters most is the **relevance** of your content. And, if it's not relevant (to readers or searchers), it simply isn't working in any case!

And, for those who may suggest the contents of Description and Keywords Tags are like magic bullets, stop! **This is simply not the case**. I say again, it's the visible words that matter most.

Alt Text

<IMG SRC="imagename.gif" WIDTH="000" HEIGHT="000" BORDER="0" **ALT**="Content is King-Writing and Editing Online">

Alternative text is inserted in the code of pages to describe image content. You can liken it to a caption the browser displays when the reader does not want to or cannot see the pictures presented in a web page. It also appears as a label when a mouse pointer is rolled over an image on a web page (Fig. 7.2).

Since many search engines consider alternative text when indexing pages, using Alt Text containing relevant key phrases can improve the search engine ranking of the page for those words.

NOTE

Alt Text is also important from an accessibility perspective. This is because computers cannot interpret images and present them in a meaningful, alternative format.

Alternative text, therefore, gives the computer something to present to the user. This is important for users who have turned off image-loading in their web browsers, those using text-based browsers, and people who are blind and require the use of a screen reader to read the contents of the screen.

More information on accessibility can be found within the website of The World Wide Web Consortium (W3C) at: http://www.w3.org/

You can also use **Bobby**™, a comprehensive web accessibility software tool designed to help expose and repair barriers to accessibility and encourage compliance with existing accessibility guidelines:
http://bobby.watchfire.com/

[Fig. 7.2]
Alt Text on the MediaCo front page.

Of course, you will only be able to influence this if you know what images are going to be used with your copy.

Off the page factors

In a further bid to deliver relevant results, search engines also consider various off the page factors. They include:

- inward and outbound links;
- click-through measurement.

The **click-through measurement** is the assessment of what pages are selected from the results of a particular search. If some high-ranking pages aren't frequently attracting clicks, they may be dropped in favour of others that do attract clicks.

This will be beyond your control other than by being influenced by your choice of Title Tag content (what the user sees within the link at the top of your listing).

However, you may be able to **influence the inbound and outbound links** – what sites are being linked to or from (in terms of quality and relevance) and the text used within those links (meaningful and usefully descriptive content).

This is, currently, particularly important with Google, which uses links as part of its PageRank assessment (the system is uses for ranking web pages).

From Google:

'PageRank relies on the uniquely democratic nature of the web by using its vast link structure as an indicator of an individual page's value.

'In essence, Google interprets a link from page A to page B as a vote, by page A, for page B. But, Google looks at more than the sheer volume of votes or links a page receives; it also analyses the page that casts the vote.

'Votes cast by pages that are themselves "important" weigh more heavily and help to make other pages "important" '.

However, while off-the-page factors may always have some influence as the search engine sands shift (try saying that quickly!), the true and focused content of your web site will win through.

That is, so long as relevancy matters more than payment for position.

Summary

When you first picked up this book, you may not have considered writing for search engines. However, by following the items above, you will have increased the likelihood of your web page content being found by searchers and, therefore, increased the likely number of readers.

Web links

Search Engine Watch (www.searchenginewatch.com)

Search Engine Watch editor Danny Sullivan is widely regarded as one of the world's foremost search engine experts. His website and newsletter are packed with useful information.

The Search Engine World (http://www.webmasterworld.com/category3.htm)

Forums covering all aspects of search engine promotion.

Checklist – writing for search engines

[ ] Have I conducted keyphrase research?

[ ] Am I targeting phrases, not single words?

[ ] Have I used keyphrases consistently throughout my copy?

[ ] Is my copy 300–500 words per page?

[ ] Have I particularly placed my key phrases within the first 150–250 characters?

[ ] Do my targeted phrases appear at the start of paragraphs?

[ ] Is the content organized logically and split into separate subject-focused pages or sections?

[ ] Have I used relevant, descriptive content within links?

[ ] Are my key targeted search phrases placed near the start of my copy?

[ ] Have I avoided being over-repetitive?

[ ] Have I created sub-headings, **emphasis** and bullet lists featuring the key phrases?

[ ] Are my key phrases placed in Title Tags (especially within the first 60 characters)?

[ ] Have I kept the important keywords at the beginning of the Description Tags and have I used 200 characters or less?

[ ] Have I used the most important keyphrases at the start of the Keywords Tags and used each keyword no more than three times?

[ ] Have I supplied Alt Text (relevant and descriptive captions for images)?

[ ] Have I identified sites to link to and provided relevant and descriptive link text?

As is your sort of mind, so is your sort of search: you'll find what you desire.

— Robert Browning

CHAPTER 8

Writing for Ads

Overview

As a multi-skilled copywriter and editor, you may be called upon to provide content for online advertisements. In many ways, the key rules covering other forms of online writing still apply.

This is because you are still trying to capture attention and provoke an action – you simply have even less space in which to do so!

Chapter objectives

The key forms of online advertising are covered within this chapter. Through the narrative, examples and tips, you should gain a better understanding of each and how to use your words effectively to gain sought-after results.

Chapter structure

- Introduction
- Pay-Per-Click search engine advertising
- Ezine/Newsletter ads
- Banners and other graphical ads
- Affiliate programs
- Summary
- Checklist.

Introduction

Online advertising takes multiple forms, from sponsored listings in Google to ads in email newsletters to banners and rich media.

While some are more visual than others, it is still the words that matter most often if readers' attention is to be captured and then converted into actions.

In addition, the online world is awash with text-only ads (from search engine results to email ads) and it takes a good copywriter to successfully stand out from the crowd in this competitive space.

Pay-Per-Click search engine advertising

Pay-Per-Click (PPC) advertising refers to the listings you usually see above or beside the main results when you are using a search engine. Often they will appear under a 'Sponsored Links' header (Fig. 8.1).

They also appear in the web search results that are presented by Pay-Per-Click providers' partner sites and within shopping-style business directories.

Leading Pay-Per-Click providers include Google, Overture and Espotting.

[Fig. 8.1]
A search on Google (UK) using the phrase 'share trading' resulted in this pay-per-click ad from Ample being presented in the right-hand column.

In some ways, it could be likened to classified advertising with a twist – the twist being that, each time someone clicks on the ad link, there is a cost to the advertiser.

How it works is as follows:

- You create your own ads (titles and descriptions).
- You choose relevant keywords and phrases which you wish to match to your ads (so the appropriate ads appear when your words or phrases are entered as a search phrase).
- You place bids against your keywords and phrases (how much you're prepared to pay per click).
- The higher your bid, the higher your ad will appear in the results.
- Each time someone clicks, you incur your bid cost.

This should **not be seen as a substitute** for your copywriting and optimization effort to achieve high positioning within the organic search results (the ones that appear within the main part of the screen and which are primarily influenced by the relevancy of your site's content).

Rather, in most cases, it should be regarded as **complementary activity**, particularly if you are:

- targeting heavily saturated keyphrases (those which many compete for);
- seeking immediate results;
- unable to optimize website content for specific words or phrases.

A big advantage of using PPC is that you pay only for a click from the ad to your website. This is a **guaranteed qualified lead** – someone has typed in the search term and will click because that is what they are actually looking for! (As opposed to generally surfing.)

But there lie your challenges:

1. To create an ad which generates responses.
2. To create an ad which generates as many **quality responses** as possible (from readers who are likely to perform your desired actions).
3. To create an ad which generates as many quality responses as possible and as few **untargeted responses** as possible (for example, readers seeking free information rather than wishing to purchase services).

Most large organizations tend to use specialist agencies to manage their PPC campaigns. For example, at MediaCo, we manage the PPC campaigns for the likes of DoubleClick, ICS Learn, Cellhire and Brother.

A fully managed service includes the following:

- Keyword research.
- Campaign planning (including cost projections).
- Keyword targeting (maximizing the effectiveness of the spend).
- Creative services (sometimes for many hundreds of ads).
- Bid and position management.
- Conversion tracking.
- Analysis and reporting.

The keyword targeting is particularly important. For example, if you chose '**golf**' as a keyword, you could end up receiving **costly clicks** from people seeking:

- a Volkswagen Golf;
- a shop selling golf clubs;
- a golf course in Scotland;
- a guide to playing better golf;
- And so on . . ..

The secret of a successful PPC campaign and, therefore, a strong conversion rate is to use **targeted phrases** – with **meaningful titles** and **descriptions**.

Bid management is also a key area. For example, if you are competing with others, you can find you are at Position One at 9.00 am but, by 9.05, you have been outbid and knocked off the first page of results.

In addition, you **may not** wish to be the highest bidder but still appear in the top three positions.

And the agency (or yourself, if you wish to get into the finer details) will also use a variety of keyword matching techniques. For example:

- **Broad matching**.
  If you enter a particular phrase and searches include your chosen words in any position, your ad will be shown.
- **Exact matching**.
  Your ad is only shown when the reader searches on your phrase exactly and no other words are included.
- **Phrase matching**.
  This reveals your ad when a search includes your phrase exactly whether or not it is surrounded by other words.

So, it can become **quite sophisticated** and **time-consuming**. However, if you're taking your first steps or are considering a relatively small campaign in terms of budget and quantity of phrases, you can do it yourself.

And, even if using an agency for campaign management and reporting, you may still prefer to collaborate regarding the creative content of the ads – you're the expert in your business after all!

So . . .

The creatives . . .

Here are my **Top 10 Tips**:

1. **Include your keywords in the text and/or title of your ads**.
   By doing so, your readers will see the words and, therefore, appreciate the relevance to their search terms. In a study, Overture found that listings that include the search term in both the title and description have a higher click-through rate (more than 50 per cent higher on average).

   Example:
   Buy a Two-Way Radio – **Two-way radios** and accessories including batteries, chargers, headsets and more. Visit **Two Way** Accessories today.
   www.twowayaccessories.com

2. **Write clearly and simply**.
   Simple language and short, non-repetitive sentences work best.

   Example:
   Catering Courses
   Get ready to taste success with
   this ICS home study course.
   www.icslearn.co.uk

3. **Reveal the attractive aspects of your offering**.
   What it is. Its benefits. Why it's better.

   Example:
   HR Payroll Software – Innovative HR **Solutions** for all your personnel, recruitment, training, **payroll** and e-HR needs. Improve your business performance with an HR management information system from ASR.
   www.asr.co.uk

4. **Be objective and informative**.
   As with other aspects of writing for the web, there is no place (or space!) for hype.

Example:
Free Visio Label Plugin
From Brother – Official Microsoft
Office System Launch Partner
www.p-touchsolutions.com

5. **Avoid superlatives.**
Greatest, Biggest, Best, etc.

Example:
Villas in South of France
Choose a quality villa from a wide
range of French destinations.
www.bowhills.co.uk

Rather than:
Villas in South of France
Bowhills have the biggest
range of French destinations.
www.bowhills.co.uk

6. **Use attention-grabbing words**.
Free, New, Win, Offer, etc. are fine if they are not misleading.

Example:
Win Great Prizes
Guaranteed prize vouchers for
every completed survey.
www.vouch4me.co.uk

7. **Be descriptive**.
Making sure the readers know exactly 'what is inside the packet'.

Example:
E-Mail **Marketing Solutions** – DoubleClick – customised email **marketing** programmes. You define the strategy, objective or programme requirement, and DoubleClick will create a system tailored to your business.
emea.ie.doubleclick.net

8. **Use a clear call-to-action.**
   So your readers know what to do and why.

   Examples:
   Health and fitness advice for **Scotland** – Find out about eating for good health with healthyliving. Click here for healthy eating and fitness advice.
   www.healthylivingscotland.gov.uk/

   Buy Maps and Travel Books at Stanfords – Stanfords **map** and travel book shop offers a wide range of world **maps** and guide books. **Buy map** and travel books at Stanfords **map** and travel book shop.
   www.stanfords.co.uk

9. **Make every word count.**
   Space is very limited so you should spend time honing your ads.

   Example:
   Buy a planter from Eden
   Supplier of quality garden vases, watering cans and planters.
   www.edenoriginal.com

10. **If relevant, be location-specific.**
    So, if you only sell products locally, say so.

    Example:
    Executive Car Hire – Chauffeur driven cars from Home James. Whether its business or pleasure hire a chauffeur driven car and let Home James transport you in style. Based in the **Midlands**.
    www.homejames.org.uk

TIP When possible, try to ensure the link goes through to a page that's relevant to the search phrase rather than a generic page.

Web links:

Google AdWords
http://www.google.co.uk/ads/

Overture
http://www.content.overture.com/d/?mkt=uk

Espotting
http://www.espotting.com

Ezine/Newsletter Ads

In the Writing for email chapter I wrote that, if content is king, nowhere is this more obvious than within the email marketing arena. Permission-based email marketing is the killer application, if used **correctly** and **creatively**.

And the same is true of advertising within Ezines and Newsletters.

People subscribe to receive these regular emails because they are **genuinely interested** in the subject matter. That makes them a **very focused** readership and ideal for targeting if you are offering related products, services or information.

For text ads, here are my **Top 10 Tips**:

1. Use one topic per ad.
2. If possible, include an offer.
3. Emphasize the benefits you offer (what's in it for them), not the features.
4. Make sure your offering fits with the theme of the Ezine or Newsletter.
   (That is, it should match the niche interest of its readership or appeal to its wider audience as a whole.)
5. Request and follow copy length and depth guidelines.
   (Frequently, standard email text ads need to be no more than 60–65 characters wide and four–five lines deep.)

6. Use a complete URL in a text link so that it can be clicked or directly copied from any email client. (That is, http://www.media.co.uk and not www.media.co.uk.)
7. Write effective headlines that convey your strongest benefits.
8. Include strong emotional words in your headlines. (For example, Discover, Secret, Free, Announcing, Easy, Special, Learn.)
9. When appropriate, inject urgency into your headlines.
   (That is, Take Action Now!)
10. Follow Tips 2–10 in the Top 10 Tips for Pay-Per-Click ads.

Here's an example of a Standard Ad:

Discover the Secrets of Effective Online Copywriting – today!

Advice, tips, examples, checklists, more . . . Content is King – Writing and Editing Online. The guide for marketers, copywriters, editors is available now. From websites, to email, search engines and ads – learn best practice and improve your skills. PLUS: Save 10% online today . . .
http://www.fullurlinhere.com

TIP

To ensure you do not exceed the 60–65 characters limit per line, it's useful to insert 65 characters across the top of your copy. Like this:

```
1234567890123456789012345678901234567890123
4567890123456789012345
```

When your copy is nearing the end of the line, insert a hard return to start a new one.

There are usually three kinds of ads available within Ezines and Newsletters:

1. **Standard, classified-style ads.**
   They are often strung together or used to break up the flow of the main body content. They tend to have a header like /// ADVERTISEMENT \\\
   Most often, they're **least effective**, as readers tend to skip past or ignore them.
2. **Sponsor ads.**
   As the sponsor of the Ezine or Newsletter, your ad will appear at the top of the copy. It is usually longer than a standard ad and, also, has a stronger association with the content as a whole. This results in a **greater number** of click-throughs.
3. **Editor's Recommendations** or **Featured Products/ Services.**
   They **work best of all** due to the fact they are fully integrated with the editorial content. They are also longer again and, in addition, it appears the publisher is saying to the reader 'We think you should look at this'!

   Sometimes you can also negotiate a free insertion of this kind of ad by offering the publisher the same opportunity within your own Ezine or Newsletter.

The tips above will deliver benefits to you whether your ads are appearing within Plain Text or HTML emails. However, HTML format also provides additional opportunities to capture your targeted readers.

For example, you can provide **attention-grabbing** logos and graphics or, if space is allowed and the functionality exists, embedded response forms and surveys.

Rich media (animations, Flash movies, etc) may also be possible.

But the **most important consideration** is that the readership matches your target market and that you provide them with content in whatever format they are used to receiving and responding to.

Banners and other graphical ads

The first banner ad appeared on *Wired Magazine's* HotWired website in October, 1994.

It is said the shape and size were selected to fit in best with the site's design and, while it was slightly larger, led to the first standard (468 pixels wide × 60 pixels deep) (Fig. 8.2).

Since then, a large variety of formats have emerged and the **voluntary guidelines** from The Interactive Advertising Bureau (IAB) include:

- Five Rectangles and Pop-Ups.
- Eight Banners and Buttons.
- Three Skyscrapers.

The IAB is also recommending a set of rich media advertising unit guidelines for **in-page** and **out-of-page** advertising (for example, floating ads or transitional pages).

The IAB site can be found at:
http://www.iab.com/

To you, the creator of the words, this provides a range of opportunities to capture readers' attention and call them to action.

[Fig. 8.2]
The first standard banner ad size – 468 pixels × 60 pixels.

As James Randolph Adams said:

> *Great designers seldom make great advertising men, because they get overcome by the beauty of the picture – and forget that merchandise must be sold.*
>
> Of course, the most effective ads combine the skills of the **copywriter** with those of the **designer** and, today, often the **multimedia developer**, too.

However, some golden rules apply in all cases. They include:

- **Know your product or service**.
  What is it you are trying to 'sell' and what are the strongest benefits it offers? You should write a list for reference.
- **Identify your objective.**
  What is the goal? For example, is it brand awareness building, sales or subscriptions?
- **Identify the key things you wish to communicate**.
  That is, what are the messages you wish to deliver?
- **Know your target market**.
  Build a picture of those who will see the ads and then consider the tone and style that would be most effective for them.
- **Find out what works already**.
  Look at the site where your ad is to appear or sites which cater for your target market. See what others are doing already.

With regard to your **written content**, here are my **Top 5 Tips**:

1. **Keep it simple.**
   Simple and direct language works best, particularly bearing in mind you only have some 2 seconds to capture your reader's attention.

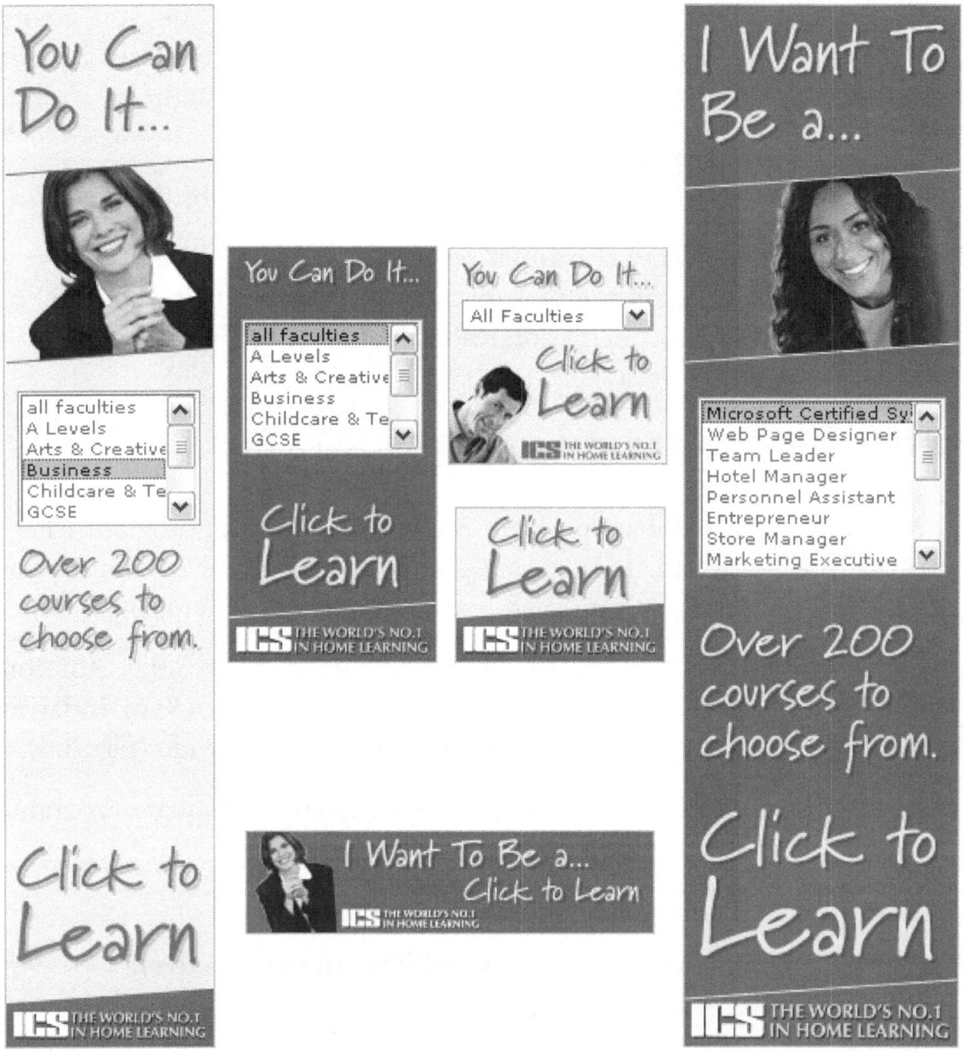

[Fig. 8.3]
A set of ads created to encourage uptake of the ICS Learn distance learning courses. http://www.icslearn.co.uk

2. **Keep it short.**
   Use the lowest number of words and characters to encapsulate your message.
3. **Provide an incentive.**
   If you're going to take readers' attention away from the main content of the page, you require to make it

worth while for them. For example, are you giving something away for free or what is the main benefit the reader will receive by clicking through?

4. **Include a clear call to action**.
   Make sure they know to 'Click Here' or there.

5. **Whet the appetite.**
   If you can capture curiosity (without being obscure) or provoke desire, readers are more likely to click.

Affiliate programs

An affiliate program is a **revenue sharing** program where an affiliate (associate/partner) website receives commission for delivering sales, leads, or visitors to a merchant website.

The first of its kind is believed to be the Amazon Associates program, which was started in 1996. Today, it has more than 900 000 members world-wide (Fig. 8.4).

In most cases, advertising material for Affiliate Programs takes three forms:

1. Banner ads (least effective).
2. Text descriptions and links (more effective).
3. Product Feeds (most effective).

The same rules as previously described for Banner Ads, Pay-Per-Click and Ezine ads should be followed when creating content for affiliate program advertising.

[Fig. 8.4]
Amazon's affiliate program was launched in 1996.

Your affiliates will decide for themselves which combinations they wish to use within their campaigns.

It is also recommended that you **refresh these items** from time to time so your affiliates' ads don't become stale.

A **Product Feed** is a database-friendly file containing information on multiple products, at the very least including fields for product name, descriptions, pricing and direct links.

It is often **regularly updated** and allows affiliates to present full product catalogues that can be browsed or searched.

Owing to the fact the content is **very specific** and that deep links are provided directly to the product in question, click-through rates and conversions are higher.

As a copywriter, your **key challenge**, once again, is to create compelling, short titles and descriptions that will help boost uptake.

Summary

In all forms of writing and editing online, our main aim is to **attract attention** and **provoke an action**, most often using as few words as possible.

Never is this more true than with advertising content. In many ways, it's the **most difficult challenge** as space is extremely limited and we are competing with the main content as well as other advertising.

For example, at first glance, you may have thought creating the content of Pay-Per-Click ads was a simple task.

However, to use the **right words** in the **right place** within the **character-count** restrictions is a craft in itself and, in most cases, multiple edits are required.

So, I hope you now feel better equipped for your frays into the advertising space and that your copywriting will be stronger whatever the form of ad you're creating.

Checklist – writing for ads

For Pay-Per-Click:

[ ] Have I created a comprehensive list of relevant keyphrases?

[ ] Are there more keyphrases that I should add for quality targeting?

[ ] Are there any keyphrases I should remove owing the fact they are too generic or off-topic?

[ ] Do my ads include the keywords in the title and/or text?

[ ] Have I written clearly and simply?

[ ] Are the attractive aspects of my offering made clear?

[ ] Is my content objective and informative?

[ ] Have I avoided superlatives?

[ ] Have I used attention-grabbing words?

[ ] Does my content clearly describe the offering?

[ ] Have I included a clear call to action?

[ ] Does every word count or can the content be further edited?

For email:

[ ] Have I used just one topic per ad?

[ ] Have I included an offer?

[ ] Does my content emphasize benefits rather than features?

[ ] Does my content fit with the theme of the email and appeal to the readers' interests?

[ ] Have I followed copy length and depth guidelines?

[ ] Have I used complete URLs?

[ ] Do my headlines convey the strongest benefits?

[ ] Have I included strong, emotional words in my headlines?

[ ] Is it possible to also inject urgency into my headlines?

[ ] Have I also followed the tips for Pay-Per-Click ads?

For banners:

[ ] Have I compiled a list of the strongest benefits my offering can deliver?

[ ] Have I identified my key objective?

[ ] Do I know the key things I wish to communicate?

[ ] Do I know the profile of my target market?

[ ] Have I assessed what others are doing?

[ ] Is my copy simple and direct?

[ ] Have I used the lowest number of words and characters?

[ ] Is an incentive offered within my ad copy?

[ ] Have I included a clear call to action?

[ ] Have I captured curiosity or provoked desire?

For affiliate programs:

[ ] Have I answered the questions above related to Pay-Per-Click, email and banner ads?

[ ] Have I created a schedule for refreshing the ads?

[ ] Can I provide content for a product feed?

Many a small thing has been made large by the right kind of advertising.

— Mark Twain

CHAPTER 9

Online Writing – the Variety Show

Overview

To be a successful online copywriter or editor, you have to be something of a chameleon, changing the colour of your text depending on the audience and objectives.

From business to business website content to short text messages, you will adopt different styles and personalities.

Once you master the various approaches, you'll find that this character shifting is one of the most interesting and rewarding aspects of writing online.

Chapter objectives

The aim of this chapter is to introduce you to various other opportunities you may encounter when writing and editing online. And to provide guidance on the best approaches to help you to achieve your sought-after results.

Chapter structure

- Introduction
- Business to Business (B2B) and Business to Consumer (B2C)
- E-commerce
- Copywriting for catalogues
- Blogs (web logs)
- SMS – text messaging
- Summary
- Checklist.

Introduction

The various hats you wear when writing are dictated by the nature of the organization you may be representing (as well as its aims) and the profile of your readership (as well as their needs and wants).

In addition, you regularly face restraints, depending on the task at hand. The following covers a range of writing and editing activity that will extend your repertoire.

Bundled as 'the variety show', it's rather like a multi-part role in *Stars In Their Eyes*. Tonight, I'm going to be . . .

Business to Business (B2B) and Business to Consumer (B2C)

There are many approaches which are common to Business to Business (B2B) and Business to Consumer (B2C). But there are differences, too.

For example, while in both cases hype and marketese should be avoided, the consumer will respond more actively to your copy if it also pulls **emotional strings** (with words like Free, Special, Easy, etc.) and more obviously tries to **grab the attention** (with words like Now, Sale, Win, etc.).

On the other hand, your B2B reader will respond better to strong evidence of your credibility. Most often, they are looking for more than instant gratification (for example, a one-off purchase). Rather they are seeking a **trusting** and often **long-term** relationship.

The discerning B2B reader is asking if you are:

- Honest
- Reputable
- Professional
- Able.

And they will **dig deeper** into the information you provide to find the answer to these questions and to satisfy themselves that you can deliver **sought-after solutions**.

Credibility is important to the B2C reader, too. But top of their list is:

- Do you have what I want?
- Can you give it to me now?

Further, while you will endeavour to build a picture of your typical reader within both sectors, you are likely to have more detail and focus when targeting the business reader.

For example, you might have:

- a company position,
- an area of expertise,
- a salary range,
- a knowledge assumption.

And each will influence the **tone, voice** and **style** you adopt as well as the **words** you use. You might even delve deeper and develop content for role-based sections. For example, 'Go here if you are a systems developer . . . ,' 'Go here if you are an IT manager . . .' and so on.

If it's sales you are seeking, the B2B cycle often takes much longer to complete. In B2C, the sale is often instant, perhaps after one or two quick comparisons, and you have to help make the process as **fast** and **simple** as possible.

Your business customer will often ponder and is more likely to spend time seeking answers to **questions**, consuming **deeper content** about your products or services (so you had better provide it!) and **comparing** your offering with that of others.

[Fig. 9.1]
The Argos website is targeted towards consumers.
http://www.argos.co.uk/

This is also because:

- business orders are usually of higher value,
- the business buyer is likely to be acting on behalf of a company,
- consumers make their own decisions; the businessperson may require purchase approval.

And you should bear in mind that, even if the sales process can take longer, the business reader tends to have **stronger needs**.

[Fig. 9.2]
Cisco Systems tailor their website towards the business reader.
http://www.cisco.com/global/UK/

Yes, the consumer may believe they need a new item of clothing or want a new toy, and your copy should persuade them why yours are better than available elsewhere.

But the businessperson is reading your copy because they have a more particular business-related need (for example a desire to make or save money) and, most likely, problems to solve.

If you can **anticipate their needs** and **solve their problems**, through informative rather than flowery language, you will have gone a long way to converting them to customers.

Consumers are also more responsive to brands (name drop them if you can!), while businesses will take more from the likes of **credible testimonials, case studies** and evidence of your **capabilities** or the suitability of your products.

Indeed, your writing effort related to B2C will often be focused on **closing a sale** – clickety-click! With B2B, your objectives are likely to shift to **lead generation** and **relationship building**. Both take effort but the latter takes more words.

With regard to **'hooks'**, incentives work for both sectors. However, while the consumer will respond well to free bottles of wine and 'chance to win —' offers, the business reader will often value information-based incentives.

Once again, the onus is on you to create and offer value-added content that your B2B reader will appreciate.

In addition, part of your B2B activity will be focused on delivering other business benefits to the company you represent.

For example, the more **questions** you answer online and the more **information** you provide (perhaps in white papers and case studies), the less time has to be spent offline in dealing with enquiries.

So, there are often significant differences between writing and editing for B2B and B2C. But, by developing your coat of many colours, you will be able to meet the demands of both.

E-commerce

Money, money, money . . . Aha-ahaaa . . .

Electronic Commerce – the buying and selling of products and services online via the Internet – is the raison d'être of a multitude of websites.

And, from **product descriptions** to **order confirmations**, your words become the voice of the virtual salesperson.

Get it right and those shopping baskets will be packed with goodies. Get it wrong and, whoosh, your would-be buyers will be off to another hypermarket in the blink of an eye.

The good news is the Internet is crying out for your services. The bad news is not enough online sellers currently realize this is the case. The proliferation of DIY catalogue systems and IT-led e-commerce sites are to blame.

Great functionality but someone forgot the fundamentals – **it is words that sell**!

Still, if you are fortunate enough to be involved in the content development of an e-commerce site, this at least gives you an immediate competitive advantage.

And the following will help you hone your approach and increase your sales.

Become your customer

Before you can write effective content that sells, the first thing you must do is become your customer. That is:

- Identify their needs and wants.
- Anticipate their problems and identify the solutions.

Having done that, you can begin to create your copy – always bearing in mind your customer's perspective. This content should be:

- informative, objective and, if possible, enthusiastic;
- credible and honest;
- clear and concise.

It should also make your customers believe that **your company** and **offerings are better** than available elsewhere.

That is the **why you should buy from us** bit.

Next comes **why you should buy this from us**.

The key is to particularly **focus on the benefits**, putting the customer into the action.

For example, don't say:

Our new Gizmo is 3 inches deep and features a phone, email, web access, diary and contacts book as well as being packaged with a USB cable for PC connections.

Rather, say:

The new Gizmo answers all your mobile needs.

- Slip it easily into your pocket (just 3 inches deep).
- Make and receive phone calls at the press of a button.
- Instantly access all your contacts and appointments.
- Use email and browse the web anytime, anyplace.
- Synchronize with your PC using the cable provided.

Incentives and **promises** will also help convert your reader into a paying customer.

For example:

- Order today and receive a free Gizmo case.
- Guaranteed clarity of reception throughout the UK.

And you should **answer the questions**. For example:

- Next-day delivery if ordered before 3 p.m.
- Only £XX pounds per month with nothing extra to pay.
- 12-month contract.
- Free 24-hour online support.

As well as the actual product or service details, you should also provide as much **supporting material** as possible. This includes:

- testimonials
- case studies

- how-to documentation
- at-a-glance features and benefits
- comparisons
- specifications.

While you want your customer to **see it, want it, buy it**, many will be more discerning and consume this material before deciding whether or not to go ahead with the purchase. So, within the site, you should tell them **everything they need to know**.

Of course, at all times, it should be easy to **'buy it now'**, **'make an enquiry'** or **'find out more'**. And you should ensure calls to action are included within your copy (for example, after each list of benefits).

Copywriting for catalogues

The more comprehensive e-commerce sites feature substantial catalogues. Driven from databases, this content often suffers from being drawn from pre-existing technical data and specifications.

Okay, I can see the ingredients (even if I cannot always understand them) but what does it do for me, and how?

That's what you, the virtual shop assistant, should be answering.

But, unless working on a rigid, pre-structured site, you shouldn't simply dive on in and start creating your **benefit-laced** product descriptions.

Rather, you should first consider and endeavour to influence the **content structure**. This should be organized according to logical **categories** and **sub-categories**.

And, while through search or deep link functionality, the developers should make it possible to buy with **as few**

clicks as possible, your content structure should consider the browsing buyer, too.

That is, for example:

1. Click – Introduce me to the product range.
2. Click – Describe my selected product category.
3. Click – Reveal the benefits offered by a particular product.

You can also plan for and develop content channels or hubs. For example, the leading hotel booking agency HotelConnect presents focused sections on the likes of Beach, Luxury and Shopping hotels (Fig. 9.3).

[Fig. 9.3]
HotelConnect uses content hubs to provide more information and lead customers to hotels by travel category.
http://www.hotelconnect.co.uk

As well as providing prospective customers with further information, this acts a funnel that leads them to accommodation by travel category.

NOTE

Not only do they help me as a buyer, but the top-level descriptive pages are good for search engine positioning.

This is because the descriptive pages can be static and optimized for keyphrases (search engines like this), whereas the product pages tend to be dynamic, often with software-generated URLs (which search engines dislike).

For example:
www.mysite.com/gizmos/
Is better than:
http://cgi-bin/www.mysite.com/detail/test_detailmain/4552,,115,3.html

When you reach the stage of creating your product descriptions, you're faced with the same challenge that exists when creating Pay-Per-Click or email ads (Chapter 8 – Writing for Ads) . . . you have to **emphasize the benefits** and **convert the reader** into a customer within a quite limited amount of space.

Practice – and lots of rewriting – makes perfect in this case. And you'll know you have succeeded when you are completely satisfied you've passed the **WWW test**:

1. **What this is.**
2. **Why you should buy it.**
3. **Why you should buy it from us.**

Then you're definitely writing copy that sells better!

Blogs

Blogs (or weblogs) are predicted by some to be the **next killer application** for online marketing.

It's suggested that, as email spam filters continue to block often-legitimate messages, the newsletter will be replaced by the web-based blog.

In addition, blogs can be **instantly** and **easily updated** quite often from any web-enabled device.

Simply put, a blog is a website featuring chronologically organized time-stamped content. New items, each with their own title, appear at the top as they are posted. Blog publishers can also include links to allow users to enter their own comments.

And, in the words of the Google-owned www.Blogger.com:

'A blog is your easy-to-use website, where you can quickly post thoughts, interact with people, and more.'

'A blog gives you your own voice on the web. It's a place to collect and share things that you find interesting – whether it's your political commentary, a personal diary, or links to websites you want to remember.'

'Many people use a blog just to organise their own thoughts, while others command influential, worldwide audiences of thousands. Professional and amateur journalists use blogs to publish breaking news, while personal journalers reveal inner thoughts.'

And, in Guardian Unlimited, Jane Perrone writes: 'A weblog is, literally, a "log" of the web – a diary-style site, in which the author (a "blogger") links to other web pages he or she finds interesting using entries posted in reverse chronological order.'

But blogs have more power than simply acting as online journals for self-publishing individuals.

And they can provide more than diaries for celebrities like Jamie Oliver (Fig. 9.4).

They can be **strong business** tools, too.

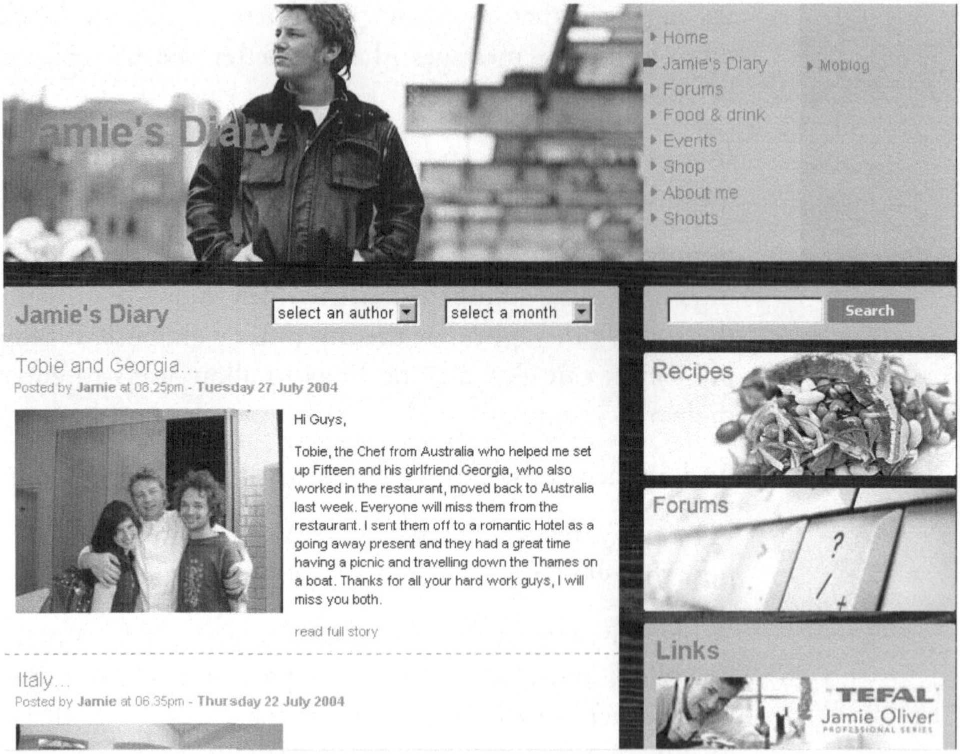

[Fig. 9.4]
Jamie Oliver's blog diary.
http://www.jamieoliver.com/diary/

And don't just take it from me. In a speech to an audience of chief executives, Microsoft chairman Bill Gates said 'Blogs are good for business!' And, love him or not, my bet's on Bill's instinct!

Gates went on to say that regular updated blogs could be a good way for firms to tell customers, staff and partners what they are doing.

And he said that blogs had advantages over other, older ways of communicating such as email.

Indeed, more than 700 Microsoft employees are already using blogs to keep people up to date with their projects.

And a survey by the Perseus Development Group found there were more than four million blogs in 2003 and there would be more than 10 million by the end of 2004.

This includes the likes of *The Guardian* (Fig. 9.5): and the Adam Smith Institute (Fig. 9.6).

Here are some of the business benefits a blog can deliver:

- Up-to-the minute information can be published for your customers.

[Fig. 9.5]
A blog from © *The Guardian*.
http://www.guardian.co.uk/weblog/

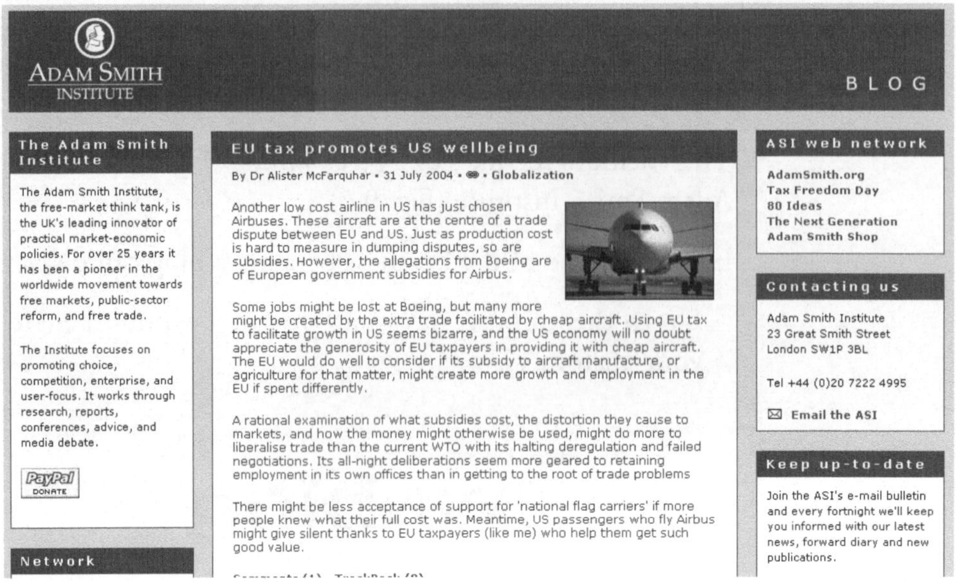

[Fig. 9.6]
The Adam Smith Institute's blog.
http://www.adamsmith.org/blog/

- Updates can be made via the Web or email.
- Higher search engine positioning can be achieved (search engines love fresh and regularly updated content).
- Other bloggers may link to your blog for free.
- Subscribers can be automatically emailed when you create a new post.
- A webfeed can be set up so readers automatically receive headings and summaries of new updates with links to the full items (these can also be picked up by aggregator services – sites which dynamically collect feeds).
- Company information can be published to keep internal staff updated (this can be password protected).

Writing for blogs

Blogs are usually written by one person in their own individual language. This, therefore, presents you with the ideal opportunity to present the **human face** and **personality** of your business.

You can be:

- conversational
- enthusiastic
- engaging
- intimate (but not overly so)
- informal.

All of this is possible without stepping beyond the limits of what would be considered as the acceptable voice of the company.

However, other styles may be required owing to the nature of your business or your readership.

On the latter, as with other forms of online writing, it's important to **know your reader** and their expectations before you begin writing a blog.

For example, your approach may be more **formal, authoritative** or **advisory**.

Or it may be appropriate for a short, sharp, news-alert style to be adopted, conveying the immediacy of your postings.

Whichever style you choose, it's important to be consistent thereafter. Multiple authors with different voices are likely to confuse your readers and reduce the effectiveness of your blog.

Short and **meaningful headlines** are important, too – not only for the reader of your blog but for those who have signed up for alerts or who are using an aggregator service.

And the **pyramid style** of writing also applies here, with the key information being presented at the beginning.

This is particularly important because an aggregator service may present only the first sentence or two of each item.

So, if you're not already, get blogging today! But, remember, once you start you have to stick with it. We have all seen sites with News sections which were 'last updated . . .' two years ago. You can't allow this to happen to your blog.

Some blog resources:

Blogger
http://www.blogger.com

Blog-City
http://www.blog-city.com/bc/

LiveJournal
http://www.livejournal.com/

Xanga
http://www.xanga.com/

Aggregator services:

Feedster
http://www.feedster.com/

Syndic8
http://www.syndic8.com/

NewsIsFree
http://www.newsisfree.com/

SMS – text messaging (TXT 2 u)

Writing SMS (Short Message Service) text messages (**writiN sms txt msgz**) may not be at the top of your list of required copywriting skills.

But **information** is one of the key items sought (and paid for) by the more than 50 million mobile-phone users in the UK.

In addition, an increasing number of organizations are successfully using SMS marketing as part of their digital strategy (Fig. 9.7).

And the uses are extremely diverse from TXT-2-WIN competitions to news services to location-based bargain alerts (for example a night-club might send text to subscribers when they are having a Happy Hour or free entry).

[Fig. 9.7]
An example of SMS marketing from Orange (http://www.orange.co.uk). How this works is as follows: a user texts 'Film' to an Orange number (or calls) and they then receive a unique code in a text message. This is their text ticket and, when shown at a participating cinema, they get two tickets for the price of one.

Here are some the key elements you should consider as a copywriter and editor for SMS activity:

- **Copy length**.

With a maximum of **160 characters** per message, this is the strongest example of the need to follow the **less is more** rule.

- **Value**.

Since a text message is very much entering your readers' personal space, it's essential you deliver **content they value** (for example, useful information or a promotion – not advertising – of interest). If you don't, you'll quickly lose their – most likely – hard-won subscription.

- **Targeting and relevance**.

The content, language and spelling you use will vary widely depending on your readership. For example, on the language/spelling front, your younger readers might respond well to 'Win a frE holidA 2 d Bahamas'. But the older reader could see that as double-Dutch.

- **Timing**.

Again saying the right thing, in the right way, to the right person, at the **right time**, to get the right results!

- **Location**.

Quite probably adding the **right place** to the above.

Abbreviations, acronyms and **emoticons** (smileys and other characters used to express feelings) are used frequently in various forms of online communication, including SMS.

Here is a small collection to get you started:

Abbreviations and acronymns

2l8	Too late
2WIMC	To whom it may concern
7K	Sick

A3	Anytime anywhere anyplace
AAMOF	As a matter of fact
AEAP	As early as possible
AFAIK	As far as I know
AFK	Away from keyboard
AKA	Also known as
AOTA	All of the above
ASAP	As soon as possible
ATB	All the best
ATK	At the keyboard
ATM	At the moment
ATW	At the weekend
B4	Before
B4N	Bye for now
BAK	Back at keyboard
BBIAF	Be back in a few
BBIAM	Be back in a minute
BBL	Be back later
BBS	Be back soon
BC	Because
BCNU	Be seeing you
BFN / B4N	Bye for now
BM&Y	Between me and you
BOL	Best of luck
BRB	Be right back
BRT	Be right there
BTA	But then again
BTDT	Been there done that
BTW	By the way

Cm	Call me
CMIIW	Correct me if I'm wrong
CMON	Come on
COB	Close of business
CU	See you
CUA	See you around
CUL	See you later
D/L	Download
Dk	Don't know
DQMOT	Don't quote me on this
DTS	Don't think so
EMA	Email address
EOD	End of discussion
EOL	End of lecture
EOM	End of message
FAQ	Frequently asked questions
FBM	Fine by me
FC	Fingers crossed
FITB	Fill in the blank
FOMCL	Falling off my chair laughing
FWIW	For what it's worth
FYA	For your amusement
FYEO	For your eyes only
FYI	For your information
G2G	Got to go
G2R	Got to run
G9	Genius
GA	Go ahead
GB	Goodbye

GFI	Go for it
GG	Good game
GL	Good luck
GMTA	Great minds think alike
GR8	Great
GSOH	Good sense of humour
GTG	Got to go
HAGO	Have a good one
HAND	Have a nice day
HF	Have fun
HOAS	Hold on a second
HRU	How are you
HTH	Hope this helps
IAC	In any case
IAE	In any event
IB	I'm back
IC	I see
ICBW	It could be worse
IDK	I don't know
IDTS	I don't think so
IG2R	I got to run
ILBL8	I'll be late
ILU	I love you
IMCO	In my considered opinion
IMHO	In my humble opinion
IMI	I mean it
IMNSHO	In my not so humble opinion
IMO	In my opinion
INAL	I'm not a lawyer

IOW	In other words
IRL	In real life
IRMC	I rest my case
IUSS	If you say so
IYKWIM	If you know what I mean
IYO	In your opinion
IYSS	If you say so
J4F	Just for fun
JAC	Just a sec
JIK	Just in case
JJA	Just joking around
JK	Just kidding
JMO	Just my opinion
JP	Just playing
KC	Keep cool
KHUF	Know how you feel
KISS	Keep it simple stupid
KIT	Keep in touch
KNIM	Know what I mean
L8	Late
L8r	Later
LOL	Laughing out loud
M8	Mate
Mob	Mobile
MTE	My thoughts exactly
MYOB	Mind your own business
NBD	No big deal
NC	No comment
NE	Any

NE1	Anyone
NFM	Not for me
NO1	No one
NOYB	None of your business
NP	No problem
NRN	No reply necessary
NW	No way
OIC	Oh I see
OMW	On my way
OO	Over and out
OOTD	One of these days
OP	On phone
OTL	Out to lunch
OTOH	On the other hand
OTTOMH	Off the top of my head
OTW	Off to work
PCM	Please call me
PDQ	Pretty damn quick
PLMK	Please let me know
PLZ	Please
PPL	People
PRT	Party
PXT	Please explain that
QIK	Quick
R	Are
RL	Real life
RME	Rolling my eyes
ROF	Rolling on floor

ROTFL	Rolling on the floor laughing
RUOK	Are you ok
SME1	Someone
SMHID	Scratching my head in disbelief
SOL	Sooner or later
SPK	Speak
SPST	Same place same time
SRY	Sorry
SUL	See you later
SUP	What's up
T2Go	Time to go
T2ul	Talk to you later
TA	Thanks a lot
TAFN	That's all for now
TAM	Tomorrow a.m.
TBD	To be determined
TBH	To be honest
TC	Take care
TGIF	Thank God it's Friday
THX	Thank You
TIA	Thanks in advance
TMI	Too much information
TMWFI	Take my word for it
TNSTAAFL	There's no such thing as a free lunch
TPM	Tomorrow p.m.
TPTB	The powers that be
TSTB	The sooner the better
TTTT	To tell the truth

TTUL	Talk to you later
TTUS	Talk to you soon
TTUT	Talk to you tomorrow
TY	Thank you
TYVM	Thank you very much
U	You
U2	You too
UOK	Are you ok
UR	You are
W8	Wait
WAM	Wait a minute
WB	Welcome back
WE	Whatever
WK	Week
WKD	Weekend
YBS	You'll be sorry
YIU	Yes I understand
YW	You're welcome

Emoticons

:-||	Angry
:-o	Appalled
:-o zz	Bored
:-S	Confused
%)	Crazy
:'-(	Crying
*:-I	Day-dreaming
_	Dazed

:-[	Despondent
:-|	Disappointed
:-#	Don't tell anyone
:-$	Embarrassed
(:-<	Frowning
$-)	Greedy
:-/	Grim
:->	Grin
:')	Happy and crying
<3	Heart
{ }	Hug
:D<	Hugs
{{{***}}}	Hugs and kisses
:^)	I don't know
:-I	Indifferent
%-}	Intoxicated
*	Kiss
:-D	Laughter
({)	Left hug
(*)¿(*)	Looking
<*_*>	Looking at you
:-}	Nervous smile
:o[	Not impressed
:-X	Not saying a word
%-6	Not very clever
-8	Note
^_^	Overjoyed
:)>-	Peace
(})	Right hug
:-(	Sad

<table>
<tr><td>:-7</td><td>Sarcastic</td></tr>
<tr><td>!:-)</td><td>Scholar</td></tr>
<tr><td>:-( )</td><td>Shocked</td></tr>
<tr><td>:-(0)</td><td>Shouting</td></tr>
<tr><td>+o(</td><td>Sick</td></tr>
<tr><td>|-I</td><td>Sleeping</td></tr>
<tr><td>|-)</td><td>Sleepy</td></tr>
<tr><td>:-)</td><td>Smile</td></tr>
<tr><td>:-)=</td><td>Smiling with a beard</td></tr>
<tr><td>:-?</td><td>Smoking a pipe</td></tr>
<tr><td>(*)</td><td>Star</td></tr>
<tr><td>: -)~</td><td>Sticking tongue out</td></tr>
<tr><td>@¿@</td><td>Stunned</td></tr>
<tr><td>B-)</td><td>Sunglasses</td></tr>
<tr><td>:-O</td><td>Surprised</td></tr>
<tr><td>: - {}</td><td>Talking</td></tr>
<tr><td>O0o:-)</td><td>Thinking</td></tr>
<tr><td>:-J</td><td>Tongue in cheek</td></tr>
<tr><td>:-&</td><td>Tongue-tied</td></tr>
<tr><td>:-)}</td><td>Trying not to laugh</td></tr>
<tr><td>:-\</td><td>Undecided</td></tr>
<tr><td>:-c</td><td>Unhappy</td></tr>
<tr><td>:-))</td><td>Very happy</td></tr>
<tr><td>8-)</td><td>Wearing glasses</td></tr>
<tr><td>:-\”</td><td>Whistling</td></tr>
<tr><td>;-)</td><td>Wink</td></tr>
<tr><td>|-O</td><td>Yawning</td></tr>
</table>

Plus, there’s an excellent and fun translation tool available from transL8it! (Fig. 9.8).

thk U & njoy :-)

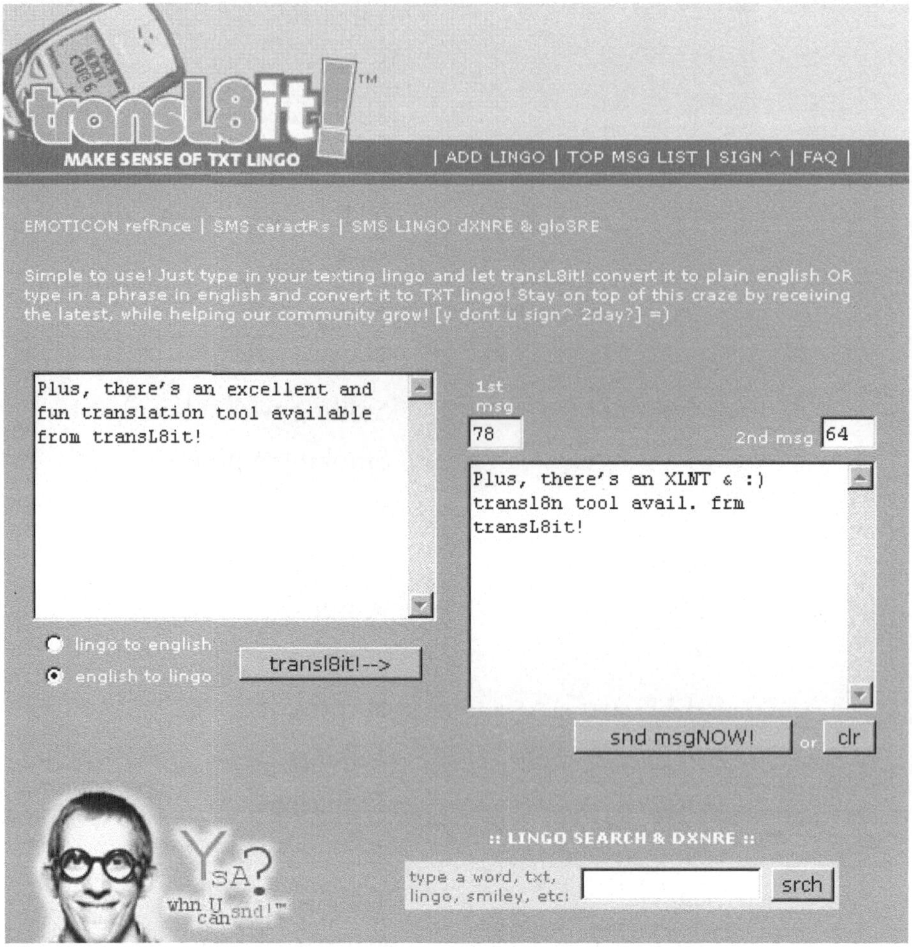

[Fig. 9.8]
The SMS translation tool available from transL8it!
http://www.transl8it.com/

Summary

They say that variety is the spice of life. That is certainly true for the online editor and copywriter. And, by mastering the many different approaches, your box of tricks will constantly amaze and the magic you weave with your words will produce stunning results.

However, as I hope you've gathered, there are also many fundamental elements to writing and editing online that are true to all projects.

These are the foundations upon which you can build your flexibility and consistently satisfy your readers and achieve your objectives.

Checklist – online writing – the variety show

Business to Business and Business to Consumer:

[ ] Have I clearly conveyed credibility?

[ ] Do I have a clear picture of my typical reader?

[ ] Is it relevant for me to develop different content for different types of reader? (B2B)

[ ] If so, have I done so?

[ ] Have I anticipated their questions and provided the answers?

[ ] Do I answer their needs?

[ ] Does my copy use words to evoke emotion? (B2C)

[ ] Have I used words to strongly capture attention? (B2C)

[ ] Does my copy help to make the sales process as fast and as easy as possible?

[ ] Have I provided suitable incentives?

[ ] Have I delivered other business benefits?

E-Commerce:

[ ] Is my content informative?

[ ] Objective?

[ ] Enthusiastic?

[ ] Credible and honest?

[ ] Clear and concise?

[ ] Have I conveyed the impression that my company and our products are better than available elsewhere?

[ ] Have I focused on the benefits offered?

[ ] Have I offered incentives?

[ ] Do I make promises that I can keep?

[ ] Have I provided as much supporting material as would be helpful?

Copywriting for catalogues:

[ ] Have I effectively influenced the structure?

[ ] Do I have logical categories and sub-categories?

[ ] Have I created content channels or hubs?

[ ] Do my product descriptions emphasize the benefits?

[ ] Have I said What It Is, Why You Should Buy It, Why You Should Buy It From Us?

Blogging:

[ ] Have I successfully conveyed the correct personality?

[ ] Is my approach suitable for the targeted readership?

[ ] Is my style consistent?

[ ] Are my headings short and meaningful?

[ ] Does the most important content appear at the start of my items?

[ ] Am I keeping my blog up to date?

SMS – text:

[ ] Is my copy short enough?

[ ] Am I delivering content that is valuable to the recipient?

[ ] Are my messages correctly targeted and relevant?

[ ] Have I used the correct language for the recipient group?

[ ] Am I sending at the best time?

Originality is not seen in single words or even sentences. Originality is the sum total of a man's thinking or his writing.

— Isaac Bashevis Singer

CHAPTER 10 Conclusions

Phew! We've covered quite a lot of ground to get to this point and I hope you've found it to be useful.

The online world provides a kaleidoscope of content opportunities and challenges. But, within the mix, there are constants.

In summary, here are the **Top 20 key points**:

1. It should be possible to quickly and easily consume content.
2. Material should be scannable, concise, intelligible, appetizing and credible.
3. The most important information should be presented at the beginning.
4. Less is more in all cases of online writing.
5. Remember the newspaper rule – Who, What, When, Where, Why, How.
6. Bullets, headings and other emphasis should be used to attract attention and guide readers throughout material.
7. Links should contain meaningful words.
8. Content should be organized into logical sections.

9. Sections should be able to stand alone.
10. In most cases, a conversation style of writing works best.
11. The active voice is much more effective than the passive.
12. You need to get to know your readers.
13. Writing requires to be in the correct tone and style for your typical reader.
14. Plain language should be used. Marketese should be avoided.
15. Readers require to know what actions to take and why.
16. Goals require to be established from the outset (what you want to achieve and what the readers want).
17. Benefits to the reader are paramount.
18. Readers' problems require to be solved and their questions answered.
19. Good writing for people is good for search engines.
20. Content should pass the AIDAS test:

    Attention (grabbing)
    Interest (strengthening)
    Desire (stimulating)
    Action (encouraging)
    Satisfaction (delivering).

The checklists are also included again at the end in the hope they'll be helpful to you as a ready reference as you progress with your writing and editing activities.

If you have any comments, questions or additional points to raise, I'd be pleased to hear from you:

david@writingediting.co.uk

I also have a little place on the Web related to this book. It's at:

http://www.writingediting.co.uk

So, thank you for your time and good luck with your writing and editing online . . ..

Checklists

Copywriting for online

[ ] Can my key content be quickly and easily consumed?

[ ] Is the most important information at the start of my copy?

[ ] Have I enhanced the readers' experience?

[ ] Will my copy keep readers engaged?

[ ] Have I written in such a way as to gain the desired actions?

[ ] Will my copy deliver the objectives?

[ ] Have I answered the questions Who, What, When, Where, Why, How?

[ ] Have I included article summaries?

[ ] Have I organized content in an easy-to-follow and intuitive structure?

[ ] Is my material broken up into shorter-than-print, logically organized sections?

[ ] Have I started articles with the conclusion, followed by the most important information and ended with the background (pyramid style)?

[ ] Is each of my sections capable of standing alone?

[ ] Have I used pointers and links to assist navigation between sections?

[ ] Are my sentences kept to about 15–25 words?

[ ] Have I used one idea per sentence?

[ ] Are my paragraphs kept to no more than four sentences, and preferably two?

[ ] Do my paragraphs only contain sentences that relate to each other?

[ ] Have I used logical transitions between paragraphs?

[ ] Have I effectively used headings, sub-headings, bullets, **emphasis** and *highlighting*?

[ ] Is my content likely to assist accessibility?

[ ] Have I used plain language?

[ ] Do my introductory sections make it clear what is on offer?

[ ] Does my other material describe, explain and inform simply and quickly?

[ ] Have I provided separate single-page articles for printing purposes?

[ ] Have I used elements encouraging interactivity?

[ ] Have I used a one-to-one, conversational style of writing?

The fundamentals

[ ] Do I know my reader?

[ ] Is it a business person or a consumer?

[ ] Is there more than one type of core reader?

[ ] Have I given them names or company positions to fit their profile?

[ ] Have I identified their key expectations and goals?

[ ] Do I know what they know already?

[ ] Have I used the correct tone and style of language?

[ ] Do I know what I seek or expect from my readers?

[ ] Have I written as I speak?

[ ] Will my material be seen as being credible?

[ ] Have I put the readers in the action?

[ ] Is the content interesting?

[ ] Is the content useful?

[ ] Is the content objective?

[ ] Is the content personable?

[ ] Is the content up to date?

[ ] Is the content accurate?

[ ] Is the content punchy?

[ ] Are the benefits and actions clear?

[ ] If I've used humour is it correct for the readership and on-topic?

[ ] Have I avoided the use of hype and marketese?

[ ] Have I avoided the use of jargon?

[ ] Are unfamiliar acronyms and abbreviations avoided or kept to a minimum?

[ ] Have I defined any acronyms and abbreviations that have been used?

[ ] Did I identify my readers' familiar and frequently used words and phrases?

[ ] Have I used their familiar and frequently used words and phrases?

[ ] Have I avoided the excessive use of capitals?

[ ] Have I persuaded my reader to take action?

Checklist – sub-editing

[ ] Is my content accurate?

[ ] Is my content easy to consume?

[ ] Is my content scannable?

[ ] Is my content concise?

[ ] Is my content intelligible?

[ ] Is my content appetising?

[ ] Have I checked everything that is checkable?

[ ] Is the key content at the top?

[ ] Have I written/edited to the correct length?

[ ] Has at least one other person proofread my material?

[ ] Have I printed out and read the copy on paper?

[ ] Have I used useful headings and sub-headings?

[ ] Have I used links effectively?

[ ] Do my headings and sub-headings include calls-to-action?

[ ] Do they convey personality?

[ ] Have I used consistent house style?

Website content planning

[ ] Have I accurately described the structure of the site?

[ ] Are all required elements included?

[ ] Is the structure simple and logical?

[ ] Are the sub-sections effectively organized?

[ ] Have I given the sections and sub-sections names which will make sense to my readers?

[ ] Do the names I've given effectively label their intended contents?

[ ] Have I established a goal/purpose for each page?

[ ] Have I listed the correct content for each area?

[ ] Have I created a visual tree diagram?

[ ] Have I identified the source of existing, reusable material?

[ ] Does my list reveal items which require to be newly created?

[ ] Have I estimated copy length for each item?

[ ] Are any applicable illustrations listed?

[ ] Is my workload prioritized?

[ ] Have I created a plan for different phases?

[ ] Have I created a forward-looking editorial plan?

Website writing

[ ] What are the goals?

[ ] What is the target audience?

[ ] What do my readers want?

[ ] What makes my topic (products, services, information) different?

[ ] What are the main benefits it can deliver?

[ ] Are there any secondary benefits?

[ ] Have I emphasized the benefits?

[ ] Have I made the value to the reader clear?

[ ] Have I answered the question 'What's in it for me'?

[ ] Have I answered the readers' needs?

[ ] What are my readers' questions or problems or objections?

[ ] Have I answered them?

[ ] Have I given answers before explanations?

[ ] Have I given summaries before details?

[ ] Have I given conclusions before discussions?

[ ] Did I examine competitors' sites?

[ ] Have I used the active voice?

[ ] Is my content useful, informative and credible?

[ ] Is key information easy to access?

[ ] Is key information short, sharp and easy to consume?

[ ] Is my material up-to-date?

[ ] Have I included details of any features/specifications?

[ ] In instructions, have I told the reader what to do?

[ ] Are actions, when required, simple to follow?

[ ] Does the About Us page, if present, tell the readers what can be done for them?

[ ] Have I created a Privacy Policy which is easy to read and understand while also reflecting the tone of other content?

[ ] Have I created a useful set of FAQs?

[ ] Does each page show the reader where they are located?

Writing for email

[ ] Am I clear about the objectives of my email?

[ ] Have I created something that people will anticipate [ ], open [ ], read [ ] and pass along [ ]?

[ ] Have I created an Advance Feature Plan?

[ ] Have I built a profile of my readership?

[ ] Can content be tailored to and segmented for different reader preferences and, if so, have I created different versions?

[ ] Does my email deliver professionalism [ ], value [ ], personality [ ], trust [ ]?

[ ] Will my content grab attention [ ], activate interest [ ], elicit desire [ ], call readers to action [ ], deliver satisfaction [ ]?

[ ] Have I used an effective From Header?

[ ] Have I used an effective Subject Line?

[ ] Is my body content relevant and focused?

[ ] Have I made the objectives clear?

[ ] Are the benefits to the reader obvious?

[ ] Have I stressed benefits rather than features?

[ ] Have I written in plain language?

[ ] Have I avoided jargon?

[ ] Have I used active verbs within hyperlinks?

[ ] Is the tone and personality right for the audience?

[ ] Is the tone and personality right for the subject matter?

[ ] Have I talked about the reader rather than 'me' or 'us'?

[ ] Have I used the active voice?

[ ] Have I written to the correct length?

[ ] Is the content immediately of interest?

[ ] Have I summarized the content in the first few sentences?

[ ] Have I provoked action at the beginning, in the middle and at the end of the email?

[ ] Have I delivered the promise?

[ ] Is my content accurate?

[ ] Have I written in the style of a letter and not an ad?

[ ] Has hype and marketese been avoided?

[ ] Is the content easily consumed by the skimming reader?

[ ] Is my writing consistent with the language of the website?

[ ] Have I used an effective PS?

[ ] Have I used an effective signature file?

[ ] Have I avoided the use of spam words?

[ ] Is the correct format being used?

[ ] Have I established the ideal frequency and timing?

[ ] Does my strategy comply with current legislation?

[ ] Is there another way I can successfully be more different?

[ ] Have I tested, tested and tested and made any required changes?

Writing for search engines

[ ] Have I conducted keyphrase research?

[ ] Am I targeting phrases, not single words?

[ ] Have I used keyphrases consistently throughout my copy?

[ ] Is my copy 300–500 words per page?

[ ] Have I particularly placed my keyphrases within the first 150–250 characters?

[ ] Do my targeted phrases appear at the start of paragraphs?

[ ] Is the content organized logically and split it into separate subject-focused pages or sections?

[ ] Have I used relevant, descriptive content within links?

[ ] Are my key targeted search phrases placed near the start of my copy?

[ ] Have I avoided being over-repetitive?

[ ] Have I created sub-headings, **emphasis** and bullet lists featuring the keyphrases?

[ ] Are my keyphrases placed in Title Tags (especially within the first 60 characters)?

[ ] Have I kept the important keywords at the beginning of the Description Tags and have I used 200 characters or less?

[ ] Have I used the most important keyphrases at the start of the Keywords Tags and used each keyword no more than three times?

[ ] Have I supplied Alt Text (relevant and descriptive captions for images)?

[ ] Have I identified sites to link to and provided relevant and descriptive link text?

Writing for ads

For Pay-Per-Click:

[ ] Have I created a comprehensive list of relevant keyphrases?

[ ] Are there more that I should add for quality targeting?

[ ] Are there any I should remove because they are too generic or off-topic?

[ ] Do my ads include the keywords in the title and/or text?

[ ] Have I written clearly and simply?

[ ] Are the attractive aspects of my offering made clear?

[ ] Is my content objective and informative?

[ ] Have I avoided superlatives?

[ ] Have I used attention-grabbing words?

[ ] Does my content clearly describe the offering?

[ ] Have I included a clear call to action?

[ ] Does every word count or can the content be further edited?

For email:

[ ] Have I used just one topic per ad?

[ ] Have I included an offer?

[ ] Does my content emphasize benefits rather than features?

[ ] Does my content fit with the theme of the email and appeal to the readers' interests?

[ ] Have I followed copy length and depth guidelines?

[ ] Have I used complete URLs?

[ ] Do my headlines convey the strongest benefits?

[ ] Have I included strong emotional words in my headlines?

[ ] Is it possible to also inject urgency into my headlines?

[ ] Have I also followed the tips for Pay-Per-Click ads?

For banners:

[ ] Have I compiled a list of the strongest benefits my offering can deliver?

[ ] Have I identified my key objective?

[ ] Do I know the key things I wish to communicate?

[ ] Do I know the profile of my target market?

[ ] Have I assessed what others are doing?

[ ] Is my copy simple and direct?

[ ] Have I used the lowest number of words and characters?

[ ] Is an incentive offered within my ad copy?

[ ] Have I included a clear call to action?

[ ] Have I captured curiosity or provoked desire?

For affiliate programs:

[ ] Have I answered the questions above related to Pay-Per-Click, email and banner ads?

[ ] Have I created a schedule for refreshing the ads?

[ ] Can I provide content for a product feed?

Online writing – the variety show

Business to Business and Business to Consumer:

[ ] Have I clearly conveyed credibility?

[ ] Do I have a clear picture of my typical reader?

[ ] Is it relevant for me to develop different content for different types of reader? (B2B)

[ ] If so, have I done so?

[ ] Have I anticipated their questions and provided the answers?

[ ] Do I answer their needs?

[ ] Does my copy use words to evoke emotion? (B2C)

[ ] Have I used words to strongly capture attention? (B2C)

[ ] Does my copy help to make the sales process as fast and easy as possible?

[ ] Have I provided suitable incentives?

[ ] Have I delivered other business benefits?

E-Commerce:

[ ] Is my content informative?

[ ] Is it objective?

[ ] Is it enthusiastic?

[ ] Is it credible and honest?

[ ] Is it clear and concise?

[ ] Have I conveyed the impression that my company and our products are better than available elsewhere?

[ ] Have I focused on the benefits offered?

[ ] Have I offered incentives?

[ ] Do I make promises that I can keep?

[ ] Have I provided as much supporting material as would be helpful?

Copywriting for catalogues:

[ ] Have I effectively influenced the structure?

[ ] Do I have logical categories and sub-categories?

[ ] Have I created content channels or hubs?

[ ] Do my product descriptions emphasize the benefits?

[ ] Have I said What It Is, Why You Should Buy It, Why You Should Buy It From Us?

Blogging:

[ ] Have I successfully conveyed the correct personality?

[ ] Is my approach suitable for the targeted readership?

[ ] Is my style consistent?

[ ] Are my headings short and meaningful?

[ ] Does the most important content appear at the start of my items?

[ ] Am I keeping my blog up to date?

SMS – Text:

[ ] Is my copy short enough?

[ ] Am I delivering content that is valuable to the recipient?

[ ] Are my messages correctly targeted and relevant?

[ ] Have I used the correct language for the recipient group?

[ ] Am I sending at the best time?

Index

Index